THE GREAT BOOKS

because women say so!

Chosen by Readers in More Than 300 Book Groups

1986-2002

BookWomen Center for Feminist Reading
Minnesota Women's Press, Inc.

©2003 Minnesota Women's Press, Inc.

Second Edition
ISBN #0-9712317-4-5
BookWomen Center for Feminist Reading
Minnesota Women's Press, Inc.
771 Raymond Avenue, St. Paul, MN 55114
(651) 646-3968
www.womenspress.com
books@womenspress.com

TABLE OF CONTENTS

Introduction   5

Part One: The Great Books
301 Great Books by women to read and discuss   8
"Great" because we say so!   45
Great Books for children of all ages   49

Part Two: Great Book Groups
Starting a great group   54
Growing a great group   59
Asking great questions   72

Part Three: Handy Lists
Authors   76
Genres   81
Book Awards   87

Acknowledgements   89

INTRODUCTION

Welcome to the world of Great Books!

Not the "great books" of the traditional canon—mostly books by dead white males—but the rich and exciting world of memorable books written by women, all kinds of women.

Here are our 301 Great Books, as chosen by readers who have been touched by them.

Every year we ask members of each book group conducted through Minnesota Women's Press, Inc. to select the book—of all the books they read that year—that most intrigued, inspired and stretched them, that provoked strongest response and discussion. In the 16 years from 1986 through 2002, more than 3,000 audacious participants in more than 300 groups have dared to immerse themselves in books by women and to name some as "great."

These titles have become our Great Book List. They're great because we say so!

Part One gives you the entire list, annotated, listed alphabetically by title. The Greatest of the Great—94 books that have been chosen by two or more groups—are marked by a ★ and are pictured.

In Part Two, look for stories by and about successful book groups of all kinds from around the country; you'll find many good ideas to consider for your own group. Also helpful will be the list of questions that groups have come up with to prompt lively and in-depth discussions.

Part Three recaps the Great Books, this time by author and genre; just as we deigned to define "great books" differently, we've also designated some new genres. Information on the major book prizes concludes Part Three.

We hope you find in this volume information, ideas and inspiration to stimulate both your personal reading and your book group activities.

the great books

part one:
THE GREAT BOOKS

Here they are: the 301 books designated by women readers at Minnesota Women's Press, Inc. as "Great Books." They're listed alphabetically by book title.

The Greatest of the Great—books selected by two or more groups—are indicated with a star and are pictured in the margins.

We have included the copyright date for each book. Sadly, we know that some of the books are out of print; others might be by the time you read this. (And—we can hope!—some that have been out of print may have come back into print.)

Expropriating the venerated "great books" title for ourselves was a bold step to take. If you're wondering how and why we came to do it, the tale on page 45 tells.

We believe strongly that every adult reader should have her own collection of children's books. The world of children's literature is a rich source of good reading for all ages. On page 49 we present a list of some of the "great books" for children that we encourage adults to read and enjoy.

the great books

THE GREAT BOOKS
Because we say so!

Accordion Crimes, E. Annie Proulx (1996). Beginning in the late 1800s and ending 100 years later, Proulx's story captures the immigrant experience in 20th century America through the life of a green button accordion.

Affinity, Sara Waters, (1999). An isolated young upper class Victorian woman becomes enmeshed with an imprisoned spiritualist in a notorious women's London jail.

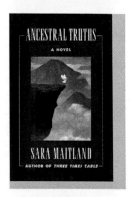

Ahab's Wife, Sena Jeter Naslund (1999). Una, the wife of Captain Ahab of *Moby Dick* fame, recounts her past, from being exiled from her Kentucky home as a child, through her adventures aboard a whaler where she meets her husband, to their life together controlled by his obsession.

★ **Alias Grace,** Margaret Atwood, (1996). This novel is based on an actual sensational murder and trial in 1843 in Canada. Did sixteen-year-old Grace Marks kill her employer or not?

Allegra Maud Goldman, Edith Konecky, (1976). Story of precocious and funny Allegra, growing up in Brooklyn from age 3 to13.

Alma Rose, Edith Forbes, (1993). Author's first novel about a woman discovering love in a small western town.

Always Coming Home, Ursula LeGuin, (1985). A utopian vision from the life story of a woman called Stone Telling.

Among Women, Louise Bernikow, (1980). A combination of literary scholarship with biography, history, politics and myth. Women talk with each other across time.

★ **Ancestral Truths,** Sara Maitland, (1993). What happened on the mountain in Zimbabwe? Clare cannot remember, even when taken home to Scotland to be with her large, loving, questioning family, where she must face the truth about her past.

★ **Animal Dreams,** Barbara Kingsolver, (1990). A woman returning to Arizona confronts her past, finds her hometown threatened by an environmental catastrophe, and reconnects with her Native American high school friend.

★ **Annapurna: A Woman's Place,** Arlene Blum, (1980). True story of the first women's ascent of one of the world's highest peaks. This account describes both the physical and interpersonal challenges the women faced.

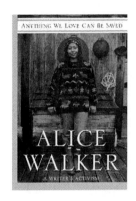

★ **Anything We Love Can Be Saved: A Writer's Activism,** Alice Walker, (1997). Walker continues to share her experiences and travels as she documents what she loves through poetry and essays.

★ **Aphrodite: A Memoir of the Senses,** Isabel Allende, (1998). The erotic world of aphrodisiacs, recipes, herbs and spices, as well as soups to have an orgy by, are described with humor in this visually colorful book.

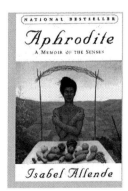

Archangel Protocol, Lyda Morehouse (2001). In a theocracy where everyone must have an interactive computer implant, an investigator takes a case that tests her faith and courage.

The Archivist, Martha Cooley (1999). At the heart of this story are T. S. Eliot's letter to Emily Hale, and the moral and ethical dilemmas that confront the archivist who oversees them not only in his work but also in his private life.

The Artist's Way: A Spiritual Path to Higher Creativity, Julia Cameron, (1992). Through a 12-week program of writing and discovery Cameron guides individuals toward honoring creativity of self.

Autobiography of a Face, Lucy Grealy, (1994). Poet Grealy's coming-of-age story as she struggled with cancer from age 9.

Backlash: The Undeclared War Against American Women, Susan Faludi, (1992). With careful documentation Faludi identifies the obstacles to women's equality. National Book Critics Circle Award, 1991.

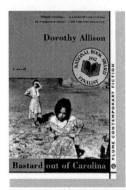

★ **Bailey's Cafe,** Gloria Naylor, (1992). A gathering at Bailey's Cafe where food is not the main ingredient but a side-dish to the magic of the human connection.

★ **Bastard Out of Carolina,** Dorothy Allison, (1992) The survival of a young girl coming of age in South Carolina surrounded by physical and emotional violence.

★ **The Bean Trees,** Barbara Kingsolver, (1988). Kingsolver's first novel introduces a heroine who "inherits" a baby, stops in Tucson when her '55 Volkswagen gives out, and becomes involved with Central American refugees.

Bee Season, Myla Goldberg, (2000). Eliza Naumann finds acceptance when she begins to win spelling bees, but her success rocks the foundation of her family. Her father gives most of his time to her brother preparing him for rabbinical studies, and her mother seems involved in her law career. But the pattern is soon to change.

Bel Canto, Ann Patchett, (2001). A novel about the connections between human beings thrust together for a period of time. Opera and the power of music are key, as Patchett explores the humanity of jungle-born revolutionaries and sophisticated international hostages. Loosely based on the 1996 take-over of the Japanese Embassy in Peru. PEN/Faulkner Award, 2002.

The Bell Jar, Sylvia Plath, (1971). Plath's only novel is based on the events of her 20th year and her struggle with questions of living and dying.

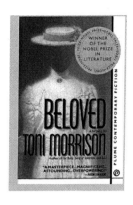

★ **Beloved,** Toni Morrison, (1987). In Ohio, after the Civil War, a mother makes heartrending choices based on her experiences as a slave. Pulitzer Prize 1988.

Bird Girl and the Man Who Followed the Sun: An Athabaskan Legend from Alaska, Velma Wallis, (1997). (See **Two Old Women,** page 40.)

Bitter Medicine, Sara Paretsky, (1988). In Paretsky's fourth mystery V.I. Warshawski, a Chicago P.I., investigates a suburban for-profit hospital where inappropriate medical practice leads to the death of a 16-year-old pregnant woman from the inner city.

Blanche on the Lam, Barbara Neely (1992). Blanche White earns minimum wage as she cleans houses for the genteel families of North Carolina. A large, middle-aged, African-American woman, feisty Blanche has a perfect vantage point for solving murders, and she does it with style.

Blood Shot, Sara Paretsky (1988). Chicago private investigator V. I. Warshawski takes on big business and chemical corruption in her old South Chicago neighborhood. As in all of Paretsky's Warshawski series, social issues predominate.

The Blue Jay's Dance, Louise Erdrich (1996). Acclaimed novelist Erdrich writes about the birth and first months of her daughter's life, reflecting on her roles as mother, writer, woman.

The Bluest Eye, Toni Morrison, (1970). Morrison's novel of a young black girl who prays for blue eyes, believing that then she would be pretty and the family life that surrounds her would be beautiful.

★ **The Bone People,** Keri Hulme, (1983). Hulme, a Maori, writes a complex novel of three outcasts in New Zealand, a woman artist, a young boy who does not speak and his Maori foster father. Booker Prize, 1985.

Bones of Plenty, Lois Phillips Hudson, (1962). Hudson depicts a proud, independent North Dakota farm family and their struggle during the Depression.

★ **Breath and Shadows,** Ella Leffland (1999). In her fourth novel, Leffland moves back and forth through three generations of a Danish family, which includes a dwarf in the early 1800s, his great-granddaughter who lives near Copenhagen in the 1880s, and her granddaughter born in Illinois and living in Switzerland. A book about inheritance, roots and myth.

★ **Cactus Thorn: A Novella,** Mary Austin, (1927). Austin's love of the southwestern desert shapes this semi-autobiographical story. Believing there is "no difference between what is social and what is personal," she weaves a tale of an eastern male politician and his connection with a self-sufficient woman of the desert.

★ **The Cape Ann,** Faith Sullivan, (1988). The 6-year-old narrator tells of her mother's desire for a Cape Ann, a house chosen from the Sears' catalogue. The story of a small Lutheran/Catholic town in Minnesota during the Depression.

Cat's Eye, Margaret Atwood, (1988). A Canadian woman in her 50s, exhibiting her controversial art, recalls vivid and haunting images of her girlfriends at age 10.

Ceremony, Leslie Marmon Silko, (1977). A young Native American returning from World War II finds he does not belong either on the Laguna Pueblo reservation or in the white community. To find himself he turns to the traditions of his Indian past.

★ **The Chalice and the Blade: Our History, Our Future,** Riane Eisler, (1987). Based on art, archaeology and history, Eisler tells a new story of our cultural origins.

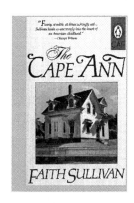

Chamber Music, Doris Grumbach, (1980). A 90-year-old widow recalls her marriage to a famous American composer, her care of him in his illness, and her joyous connection to Anna, as she founds a community for aspiring artists, in tribute to her husband.

★ **The Changelings,** Jo Sinclair, (1955). Coming of age in the '50s, two young friends, one black, one Jewish, face the anger and hostilities that result from the integration of their neighborhood.

Child of Silence, Abigail Padgett (1993). Child-abuse investigator Bo Bradley is assigned to the case of a young boy abandoned near an Indian reservation. Her manic-depressive personality provides important discoveries as she protects the boy.

Children of God, Mary Doria Russell, (1998). A return mission to the planet of Rakhat in this sequel to The Sparrow is centered around the consequences of the actions of the first mission. In this book Russell further explores religious freedom, conscience, and long, skinny fingers.

A Chorus of Stones: The Private Life of War, Susan Griffin, (1992). In this part autobiography and part history, Griffin writes of individual lives affected by wars, as she explores the function and meaning of war.

Circle of Stones: Woman's Journey to Herself, Judith Duerk, ed., (1989). A journey to the Feminine through stories, dreams and visions of women.

A Cold Day for Murder, Dana Stabenow (1992). This is the first book in Edgar Award-winner Stabenow's series featuring Kate Shugak, who solves murder and mayhem across Alaska.

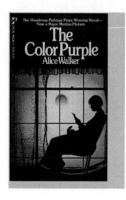

Cold Sassy Tree, Olive Ann Burns, (1984). Small-town Southern life in the early 1900s about coming of age and the ties that bind families together.

Color of Distance, Amy Thomson (1999). Marooned in an uninhabitable rainforest populated by an amphibian species, a woman's only hope is to assimilate. This is a tale of two heroines, one human, one not.

★ **The Color Purple,** Alice Walker, (1982). Novel of the difficult coming-of-age of a young woman in Georgia who finds the courage to love and to laugh after meeting her husband's female lover, a flamboyant blues singer. Pulitzer Prize 1983, National Book Award 1983.

Confessions of Madame Psyche, Dorothy Bryant, (1986). An orphan, growing up in San Francisco, fakes a vision of houses falling just before the great earthquake of 1906. Known as Madame Psyche, she travels to Europe and becomes a mystic.

Copper Crown, Lane Von Herzen, (1992). Debut novel about violent racism in rural Texas in 1913 and the friendship of two young women, one white and one black.

The Creation of Patriarchy, Gerda Lerner, (1986). Historian Lerner looks back at the origins of the collective dominance of women by men.

The Crone: Woman of Age, Wisdom and Power, Barbara Walker, (1985). An affirmation of the wisdom of older women.

Crucial Conversations, May Sarton, (1980). A long-time marriage ends when a wife decides to leave her husband.

Dakota: A Spiritual Geography, Kathleen Norris, (1993). Observations and contemplations by poet Norris, who moved from New York City back to her girlhood home in a small South Dakota town.

Dark Nantucket Noon, Jane Langton, (1986). One of Langton's mystery series featuring Homer Kelly. A murder takes place on Nantucket Island during an eclipse and Kelly sets out to find the culprit.

Daughter of Earth, Agnes Smedley, (1929). Smedley's only novel, based on her life from a poor Missouri childhood in the 1890s to her death in China in 1950.

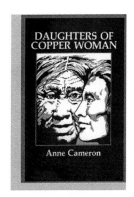

Daughter of Elysium, Joan Slonczewski, (1993). Raincloud and her husband Blackbear visit Elysium to learn of Elysians' greatest accomplishment: immortality.

The Daughter of Time, Josephine Tey, (1951). Inspector Alan Grant of Scotland Yard becomes fascinated with a portrait of Richard III and wonders whether he really was a villainous man of history or…was there more to the kind of man Richard Plantagenet really was.

Daughter of the Queen of Sheba, Jacki Lyden, (1998). A memoir by the daughter of a manic-depressive mother. A poignant story of survivors.

★ **Daughters of Copper Woman,** Anne Cameron, (1981). A retelling of Northwest coast Indian myths shared with Cameron by native women of Vancouver Island.

★ **Death Comes for the Archbishop,** Willa Cather (1927). A fictionalized account of the life of mid-19th century Santa Fe Archbishop Lamy, portrayed by Cather as Father Latour. Latour and his friend and fellow priest, Father Vaillant, work to win the Southwest for Catholicism.

The Devil's Chimney, Anne Landsman (1997). This novel explores race and gender in rural South Africa as Connie Lambrecht, dazed by alcohol and memory, becomes obsessed by 90-year-old stories of the disappearance of a young girl in a passage called the Devil's Chimney and an upper-class woman who runs an ostrich farm.

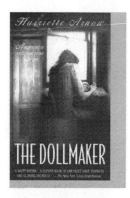

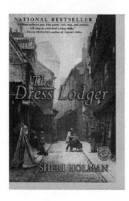

Diary of a Zen Nun: Everyday Living, Nan Shin, (1986). The author, struggling with ovarian cancer, finds hope through Zen as she writes of life and death.

Different Daughters: A Book by Mothers of Lesbians, Louise Rafkin, ed., (1987). Twenty-five mothers write about the essential questions mothers of lesbians confront.

Different Mothers: Sons and Daughters of Lesbians Talk About Their Lives, Louise Rafkin, ed., (1990). Children of lesbians share their stories. Lambda Award 1990.

★ **The Dollmaker,** Harriette Arnow, (1954). A Kentucky mountain woman, who creates beautiful wood carvings, is uprooted from her backwoods home when her husband moves the family to wartime Detroit to find work.

Down the Wild River North, Constance Helmericks, (1989). Helmericks and her teenage daughters canoe down the Peace, Slave and MacKenzie rivers.

★ **Dreaming the Dark: Magic, Sex and Politics,** Starhawk, (1982). Starhawk's message of hope for healing self, the community and even the planet.

Dreaming of the Bones, Deborah Crombie (1997). A literary mystery in which Scotland Yard Superintendent Duncan Kincaid is off to Cambridge at his ex-wife's request to look into a long-ago suicide.

★ **The Dress Lodger,** Sheri Holman (2001). The lives of 15-year-old prostitute, Gustine, and a surgeon who needs corpses for his medical school, are tied together in this story set in 19th-century England. Cholera is spreading through the town and Gustine turns to the surgeon to help save the life of her child.

★ **Drinking the Rain,** Alix Kates Shulman, (1995). Writer Shulman lives in solitude on a Maine island six months of every year. This is the story of what led her there and held her over the years.

The Driver's Seat, Muriel Spark, (1994). Does this woman's bizarre behavior invite her death?

The Education of Harriet Hatfield, May Sarton, (1989). At age 60, Harriet Hatfield opens a bookstore for women in a blue-collar neighborhood of Boston.

The Edge of the Sea, Rachel Carson, (1955). Carson's careful observation of sea life along the Maine coast over many years is described, in lyrical style.

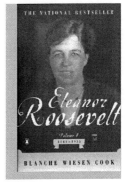

★ **Eleanor Roosevelt, Volume One: 1884-1933,** Blanche Wiesen Cook, (1992). History told around the life of a strong, dedicated woman. Lambda Award 1992.

★ **The Empress of One,** Faith Sullivan, (1996). Sullivan's fifth novel tells of Sally's growing up during the '30s and '40s in small-town Minnesota. A story of how those who differ are treated by others, some with great understanding, some with none.

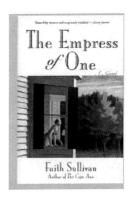

Ethan Frome, Edith Wharton, (1911). Tragedy blankets a stark Massachusetts farm as the three who live there find their lives spinning a web of sorrow from which there is no escape.

★ **Ex Libris: Confessions of a Common Reader,** Anne Fadiman, (1998). Essays around the joy of words and reading by avid reader Fadiman.

Extra Innings: A Memoir, Doris Grumbach, (1993). A journal of a year of writer Grumbach's life as she approached her 75th birthday.

Fall on Your Knees, Anne-Marie MacDonald, (1996). A multi-generational tale of four sisters who live in a family steeped in secrets and lies. Set on Cape Breton Island off Nova Scotia the story begins, "THEY'RE ALL DEAD NOW." Secrets are revealed as the novel unfolds. Winner of the Commonwealth Writers Prize for Best First Book, 1997.

The Finishing School, Gail Godwin, (1985), Viking Penguin. A teenage girl is uprooted to a new part of the country and begins a friendship with an older woman as they explore the woods together.

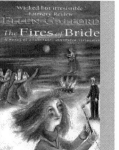

★ **The Fires of Bride,** Ellen Galford, (1986). Humorous tale about a young artist who ends up on a remote island in Scotland's Outer Hebrides, where the spiritual power of women has ancient roots.

For Her Own Good: 150 Years of the Experts' Advice to Women, Barbara Ehrenreich and Deirdre English, (1978). An analysis of 150 years of disagreement between American women and "expert" professionals, especially doctors.

Forever Ours, Janis Amatuzio, (2002). From her experiences as county coroner, forensic pathologist Amatuzio tells stories of love, compassion and understanding following the death of a loved one.

The Four-Fold Way: Walking the Paths of Warrior, Teacher, Healer and Visionary, Angeles Arrien, (1993). Anthropologist Arrien presents ways to restore the balance in ourselves and in our environment.

Frankenstein, Mary Shelley, (1818). Written when Shelley was 19, the book dramatizes the danger of presuming to create life upon a laboratory table.

The Fresco, Sheri Tepper, (2000). When a benevolent race from another world contacts an abused Albuquerque housewife, she begins a journey of danger and redemption, for both herself and Earth.

Frida: A Biography of Frida Kahlo, Hayden Herrera, (1983). The tumultuous life of Mexican painter Frida Kahlo.

★ **Fried Green Tomatoes at the Whistle Stop Cafe,** Fannie Flagg, (1987). An entertaining novel of the South told in the 1980s by an elderly woman as she reminisces to her middle-age friend. Among the highlights is the story of two women who ran the Whistle Stop Cafe in rural Alabama.

★ **Fugitive Pieces,** Anne Michaels, (1996). In this lyrical and haunting tapestry of pain and healing, a young boy's family is annihilated by the Nazis. Befriended by a Greek geologist, he works his way through sorrow, pain and loss to eventual self-discovery. Orange Prize winner.

★ **Full Tilt: Ireland to India with a Bicycle,** Dervla Murphy, (1965). Memoir by one of travel writing's most adventurous women.

★ **Gate to Women's Country,** Sheri Tepper, (1988). In this futuristic country, women raise the children and shape the culture, while warrior men live in garrisons outside the town.

Gaudy Night, Dorothy Sayers, (1935). Harriet Vane returns to Oxford for a reunion and finds herself in the middle of a mystery. Who is haunting her old college? Lord Peter Whimsey comes to help and they renew their earlier attraction to each other.

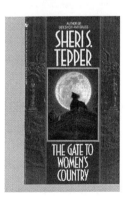

★ **Geek Love,** Katherine Dunn, (1989). A novel of an unusual carnival family which includes the grandmother who ingests drugs and other noxious things to make sure her babies are special; the daughter who is hairless and humpbacked; and the granddaughter whose only uniqueness is her tail.

Gertrude and Alice, Diana Souhami, (1991). Gertrude Stein and Alice Toklas' friendship and love from 1907 to 1957.

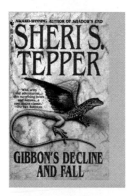

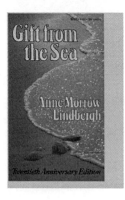

★ **Gibbon's Decline and Fall,** Sheri Tepper, (1996). In the year 2000, religious fundamentalism is sweeping worldwide. A group of women, friends for 40 years, unite to defend a 15-year-old girl. Their actions affect the future of all humanity.

★ **Gift From the Sea,** Anne Morrow Lindbergh, (1955). Lindbergh's meditations on youth and age, love and marriage, solitude and contentment, using sea shells as metaphor.

Girl with a Pearl Earring, Tracy Chevalier, (1999). In 17th-century Holland, a coming- of-age story of a fictional 16-year-old muse who might have inspired Vermeer's painting of the Girl with a Pearl Earring.

The Girl Within: A Groundbreaking New Approach to Female Identity, Emily Hancock, (1989). Psychologist Hancock identifies a turning point for women between age 10 and the onset of adolescence.

The Giver, Lois Lowry, (1993). Twelve-year-old Jonas lives in a seemingly ideal world. Not until he is given his life assignment as the Receiver of Memory does he begin to understand the dark secrets behind this fragile community. Newbery Medal winner.

★ **The God of Small Things,** Arundhati Roy, (1997). Winner of the 1997 Booker award, this first novel is of a family in southern India and the love between a man and woman of different castes.

The Goddess Celebrates: An Anthology of Women's Rituals, Diane Stein, ed., (1991). A collection of writings on rituals by women who are reclaiming Goddess-centered spirituality.

Going Out of Our Minds: The Metaphysics of Liberation, Sonia Johnson, (1987). Johnson chronicles her political journeys as well as her internal transformation.

The Great Cosmic Mother: Rediscovering the Religion of the Earth, Monica Sjoo and Barbara Mor, (1987). The authors explore the Goddess through religious, cultural and archaelogical sources.

Green for Danger, Christianna Brand, (1945). A mystery set in a military hospital during a blitz in WWII. A patient dies, a nurse is murdered, six suspects surface. Inspector Cockrill investigates.

Growing Pains, Wanda Gag, (1940). Artist Gag's diaries from her adolescence and young womanhood.

Guardian Angel, Sara Paretsky, (1982). Chicago private investigator V.I. Warshawski takes on the labor unions and politicos in this 7th in a series.

★ **Gyn-Ecology: The Metaethics of Radical Feminism,** Mary Daly, (1978). Daly, a radical feminist who combines theology, mythology, philosophy, history and medicine, makes a great leap into a-mazing space.

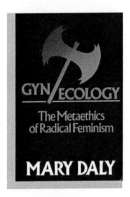

★ **The Handmaid's Tale,** Margaret Atwood, (1985). A gripping tale, set in the near future, of women's lives when all their rights are taken away.

Having Our Say: The Delany Sisters' First 100 Years, Sarah and A. Elizabeth Delany, with Amy Hill Hearth, (1993). Two centenarians recall growing up in turn-of-the-century North Carolina. This dual memoir offers a glimpse of the birth of black freedom and the rise of the black middle class.

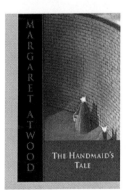

He, She and It, Marge Piercy, (1991). Piercy explores the ethical questions raised by the creation of ever-more human-like machines as she asks the question what makes humans human.

★ **Healing the Wounds: The Promise of Ecofeminism,** Judith Plant, ed., (1989). Essays, stories and poetry present a combined vision of feminist and ecological perspectives.

High Tide in Tucson: Essays from Now or Never, Barbara Kingsolver, (1995). Kingsolver writes of family, community and the natural world.

The Home-Maker, Dorothy Canfield, (1924). Traditional roles of husband and wife are reversed when the husband is confined in a wheelchair and his wife must work to support the family.

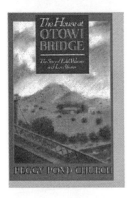

★ **The House at Otowi Bridge: The Story of Edith Warner and Los Alamos,** Peggy Pond Church, (1960). Part biography, part memoir, this is the story of Edith Warner, an Easterner who fell in love with New Mexico and settled there in the '30s, told by poet Church, who grew up in the remote area where Warner lived.

The House Tibet, Georgia Savage, (1989). Australian author writes of a young girl fleeing violence in her home, taking her autistic brother with her and joining a band of homeless children, ending up in a wondrous refuge called The House Tibet.

★ **Housekeeping,** Marilynne Robinson, (1981). A novel steeped in images of earth, water, air and fire. A family of women and a young girl's connection to her eccentric aunt.

★ **Hummingbird House,** Patricia Henley (1999). Kate follows her friend to Nicaragua and Guatemala during the mid-1980s, planning to return to the United States. When her friend is killed, Kate remains in Guatemala and becomes involved with the complex political realities of the region. This first novel was shortlisted for the National Book Award.

★ **The Hundred Secret Senses,** Amy Tan, (1995). Olivia wants nothing to do with her half sister, Kwan, who lives in a world of Chinese spirits. But when Olivia experiences changes in her personal life, Kwan brings the pieces of their sisterhood together in a journey of faith.

I Been In Sorrow's Kitchen and Licked Out All the Pots, Susan Straight, (1992). A big, Gullah-speaking South Carolina woman finds meaning in her life raising her twin sons.

I Know Why the Caged Bird Sings, Maya Angelou, (1969). The first of five autobiographical books about Angelou's difficult early life in Stamps, Ark. and St. Louis, Mo.

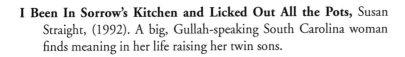

★ **In a Different Voice: Psychological Theory and Women's Development,** Carol Gilligan, (1982). Psychologist Gilligan explores women's voices and develops a female-oriented theory of moral development.

★ **In Search of Our Mother's Gardens: Womanist Prose,** Alice Walker, (1983). Essays from the '60s, '70s and '80s by poet/novelist/activist Walker, author of "The Color Purple."

In the Company of Strangers, Mary Meigs, (1991). Account of the making of the Canadian movie "Strangers in Good Company" by one of the women in the cast.

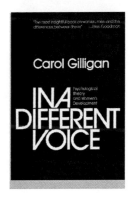

★ **In the Time of the Butterflies,** Julia Alvarez, (1994). This work of fiction honors the lives of the four Mirabel sisters, known as Las Mariposas—"The Butterflies"—who were among the leading opponents of the Trujillo dictatorship in the Dominican Republic.

An Intimate Wilderness: Lesbian Writers on Sexuality, Judith Barrington, ed., (1991). Essays, stories and poems of contemporary lesbian writers presenting a complex picture of lesbian sexuality.

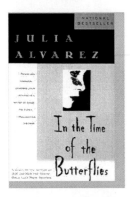

★ **Into the Forest: A Novel,** Jean Hegland, (1996). Two sisters alone in the redwood forest of California learn to survive on the land as all modern systems crumble around them.

Jane Eyre, Charlotte Brontë, (1847). This classic novel tells the story of an unforgettable heroine, the spirited and courageous orphan Jane Eyre.

★ **Janet Frame: An Autobiography,** Janet Frame, (1982). New Zealand novelist and poet's personal struggle from poor childhood, through institutionalization, to literary recognition.

★ **Journal of a Solitude,** May Sarton, (1977). Sarton writes of her 59th year and the challenges of solitude in Nelson, New Hampshire.

The Journey, Ida Fink, (1990). Two sisters escape the Jewish ghettos of Poland and with false identity papers volunteer for work in Germany.

Kindred, Octavia Butler, (1979). A time-travel tale in which a contemporary African American woman is transported back to a southern plantation where her ancestors were slaves.

Kingfishers Catch Fire, Rumer Godden, (1953). A young English woman and her family move to colonial India, encountering heartbreak as they adjust to a different culture.

The Ladies, Doris Grumbach, (1984). A fictionalized telling of the true story of two Irish women who eloped to Llangollen, Wales, in the 18th century and lived as a married couple.

Lambs of God, Marele Day, (1998). Three nuns, forgotten by the world, lead a quiet life on an isolated island where they tend their sheep. One day, a priest arrives, and a battle of wills and faith ensues.

★ **The Last Report on the Miracles at Little No Horse,** Louise Erdrich, (2001). The story focuses on a young priest, Father Damien Modeste, whom we meet briefly in earlier Erdrich books. His remarkable journey recapitulates the stories of some of the native peoples of North Dakota through memories, conversations, tales and reminiscences, shedding new light on these events, while his own story unwinds.

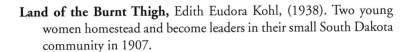

Land of the Burnt Thigh, Edith Eudora Kohl, (1938). Two young women homestead and become leaders in their small South Dakota community in 1907.

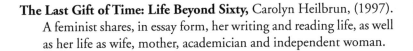

The Last Gift of Time: Life Beyond Sixty, Carolyn Heilbrun, (1997). A feminist shares, in essay form, her writing and reading life, as well as her life as wife, mother, academician and independent woman.

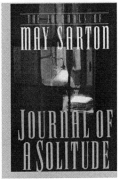

★ **Laughter of Aphrodite: Reflections on a Journey to the Goddess,** Carol Christ, (1987). Feminist theologian Christ shares her spiritual journey from Christianity to the Goddess.

★ **Letters from Yellowstone,** Diane Smith (1999). On a scientific expedition in Yellowstone Park in 1898, a young woman botanist discovers the joys of the wilderness and the passion of discovery. Winner of the Pacific Northwest Booksellers Association Award for Fiction, 1999.

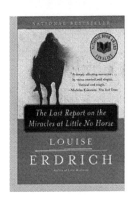

Letters to May, Eleanor Mabel Sarton, (1986). Thirty years of letters from mother to daughter, the first written when May Sarton was 3, the last, two years before Eleanor Mabel Sarton's death.

Life and Death in Shanghai, Nien Cheng, (1986). Nien Cheng's chronicle of six-and-a-half years' imprisonment in Communist China during the Cultural Revolution.

Life is Goodbye, Life is Hello: Grieving Well Through All Kinds of Loss, Alla Bozarth Campbell, (1982). A book about change, loss and healing.

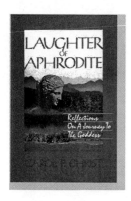

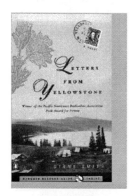

Life's Companion: Journal Writing as a Spiritual Quest, Christina Baldwin, (1990). A guide to journal writing as a means of expanding inner horizons.

Like Water for Chocolate, Laura Esquivel, (1989). Exquisitely sensuous Mexican magic.

The Little Locksmith: A Memoir, Katherine Hathaway Butler, (1943). This memoir of transformation and spiritual truth covers Butler's childhood years, which she spend strapped to a board to cure a back condition, her eventual purchase of a house and her marriage. Republished by Feminist Press.

Living in the Light: A Guide to Personal and Planetary Transformation, Shakti Gawain, (1986). Exercises, meditations and affirmations in learning to trust your creativity.

Long Walks, Intimate Talks, Grace Paley and Vera Williams, (1991). Drawings, poems and prose by writer Paley and artist Williams about peace and the celebration of each day.

The Longings of Women, Marge Piercy, (1994). Three women: an academic, a murderer, and a homeless woman, share the same longing to be valued and loved.

The Loony-Bin Trip, Kate Millet, (1990). Fiercely independent, Millet struggles with her diagnosis as manic-depressive and poses challenging questions to the medical establishment.

★ **Lost in Translation: A Life in a New Language,** Eva Hoffman, (1989). Hoffman's memoir of her early years in Poland, her teen years in Canada and her adult years as part of New York's literary world.

★ **Love Medicine,** Louise Erdrich, (1984). Saga of two Native American families across several generations, living on a reservation and in the Red River Valley of North Dakota.

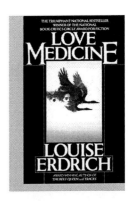

Lucy Gayheart, Willa Cather, (1935). A story of the heartache that awaits a gifted young woman who leaves her small Nebraska town to pursue a life in art.

Luna, Sharon Butala, (1988). Canadian Butala writes of prairie women and the variety of life choices they made.

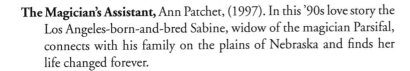

The Magician's Assistant, Ann Patchet, (1997). In this '90s love story the Los Angeles-born-and-bred Sabine, widow of the magician Parsifal, connects with his family on the plains of Nebraska and finds her life changed forever.

★ **Mama Day,** Gloria Naylor, (1988). Matriarch Mama Day calls up lightning storms on her Georgia sea island and struggles for her great-niece's life and soul, which are in danger from the island's dark forces.

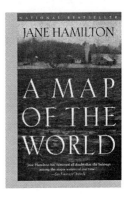

★ **A Map of the World,** Jane Hamilton, (1994). From her orchard farmhouse in Wisconsin, Hamilton writes about the precarious balance of imagined security.

★ **Maria: The Potter of San Ildefonso,** Alice Marriott, (1948). First published in 1948, this biography/oral history tells of Maria Martinez, who became one of the most famous pueblo potters, and her people.

Maternal Thinking: Toward a Politics of Peace, Sara Ruddick, (1990). Ruddick explores a feminist peace politics based on the day-to-day raising of children.

Me: A Memoir, Brenda Ueland, (1939). Autobiography/memoir of writer Ueland's experience in Minneapolis and New York during the '20s and '30s.

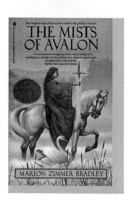

★ **Mean Spirit,** Linda Hogan, (1990). Native American poet Hogan's novel of the disintegration of the Osage Indian tribe as white men take back the Oklahoma land under which oil is discovered.

★ **The Mists of Avalon,** Marion Zimmer Bradley, (1982). The King Arthur tales told from the perspectives of the women of the time.

The Mother's Songs: Images of God the Mother, Meinrad Craighead, (1986). Craighead's paintings, with comments by the artist.

A Muriel Rukeyser Reader, Jan Heller Levi, ed., (1994). This collection gives a wide-ranging sampling of 45 years of Rukeyser's poetry, but as important are her far-seeing, informing connections between poetry and history, science, politics and ourselves.

My Antonia, Willa Cather, (1918). Literary masterpiece of an immigrant pioneer woman on the Nebraska plains.

★ **My Year of Meats,** by Ruth Ozeki, (1998). A Japanese-American film- maker is hired by a Japanese company to film American families happy to be eating beef. As she pursues the project the realities of the meat industry become something different than she started out to film. Pacific Rim Award, 1998.

Native Tongue, Suzette Elgin, (1984). Linguistics professor Elgin writes of a future world where all of women's rights are denied, even their language.

Nervous Conditions, Tsitsi Dangarembga, (1988). Zimbabwean author presents a coming-of-age story and the losses involved when one culture colonizes another.

Nickel and Dimed, On (Not) Getting By in America, Barbara Ehrenreich, (2001). Reporter Ehrenreich joins the legions of working people who struggle to get by on poverty-level wages and gives us a working-eye view of what their lives are really like.

Night Watch, Frida Sigurdardottir, (1988). As a modern Icelandic journalist sits a death watch in her mother's hospital room in Reykjavik, she reflects on the lives of her mother and aunt and their ancestors, who lived harsh lives along the sea in rural Iceland. Winner of the Nordic Council Literary Award (1988).

★ **Nine Parts of Desire, The Hidden World of Islamic Women,** Geraldine Brooks, (1995). As a news correspondent in the Middle East, Brooks set out to learn about and understand what life was like for the women of the region.

None to Accompany Me, Nadine Gordimer, (1994). In her 11th novel, South African Gordimer writes of protagonist Vera Stark, a white lawyer, who represents the blacks in their struggle to reclaim South African land. Gordimer received the Novel Prize for Literature in 1991.

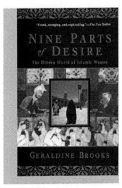

★ **North Spirit: Sojourns Among the Cree and Ojibway,** Paulette Jiles, (1995). Poet/journalist Jiles calls this work "creative non-fiction" in which "all the incidents are true." Jiles writes of her experience in northern Canada working on the only Ojibway-language newspaper in the world.

★ **Now in November,** Josephine Johnson, (1934). Johnson's first novel about a middle-class family driven into poverty by the Depression. Pulitzer Prize winner, 1935.

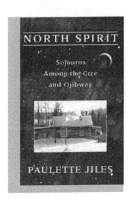

O Caledonia, Elspeth Barker, (1991). Depicts Scottish life through the fated main character, young Janet, a girl who finds solace in reading, learning and nature.

O Pioneers!, Willa Cather, (1913). Cather's first novel about the immigrants who settled the Nebraska prairie.

Odd Girls and Twilight Lovers: A History of Lesbian Life in Twentieth-Century America, Lillian Faderman, (1991). A scholarly study of outsider women whose sexuality and politics have affected mainstream America. Lambda Award 1991.

Old Books, Rare Friends: Two Literary Sleuths and Their Shared Passion, Leona Rostenberg & Madeleine Stern, (1997). For more than 60 years these two friends have shared a love of literature, becoming experts in the rare book world, and writing and editing numerous books separately and together.

★ **One True Thing,** Anna Quindlen, (1994). A successful professional woman returns to her hometown, against her wishes, to care for her dying mother.

★ **Out of Time,** Paula Martinac, (1990). A stolen scrapbook of women's photographs from the 1920s leads to exploring the connections of four women who called themselves "The Gang." Lambda Award 1990.

Outercourse: The Be-Dazzling Voyage, Mary Daly, (1992). "Containing recollections from my *Logbook of a Radical Feminist Philosopher* (Be-ing an account of my time/space travels and ideas—then, again, now and how)."

Overlay: Contemporary Art and the Art of Prehistory, Lucy Lippard, (1983). Feminist art historian Lippard connects contemporary art to prehistoric sites and symbols.

An Owl on Every Post, Sanora Babb, (1970). Memoir of a young girl's hard, but magical, life on the Colorado frontier in pre-World War I America.

Parable of the Sower, Octavia Butler, (1993). In America in 2025 the gap continues to grow between the haves and have-nots. When violence alters one young woman's protected life, annihilating her family and friends, she leads a small band of followers to the promise of a new life.

Paradise, Toni Morrison, (1997). An all-black utopia is created in small-town Ruby, Oklahoma. But what will be done about those women living in the convent outside of town?

★ **Paris Was a Woman: Portraits from the Left Bank,** Andrea Weiss, (1995). Filled with historic photos and discussion of women-owned bookstores and independent creative women on the Left Bank in Paris from 1920 to 1940, this was a documentary film before being put into book form.

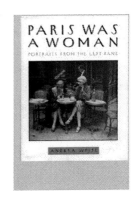

★ **Paula,** Isabel Allende, (1994). In this memoir, written as her daughter lies unconscious and terminally ill, Allende writes of her family's exile, her Chilean heritage and her love for her dying daughter.

★ **Pigs in Heaven,** Barbara Kingsolver, (1989). The story of "The Bean Trees" is continued and explores the complexity of love between mother and child across cultures.

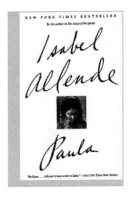

A Place Where the Sea Remembers, Sandra Benitez, (1993). A first novel of love and anger, hope and tragedy, in the Mexican village of Santiago.

★ **The Poisonwood Bible,** Barbara Kingsolver, (1998). A Baptist missionary takes his wife and four daughters to the Belgian Congo in 1959, where war is brewing. The mother and daughters write of their lives and the different ways they are marked by the father's intractable mission and by Africa itself.

Pornography and Silence: Culture's Revolt Against Nature, Susan Griffin, (1981). Griffin argues that "pornography is an expression not of human erotic feeling and desire, and not of a love of the life of the body, but of a fear of bodily knowledge, and a desire to silence eros."

★ **Possessing the Secret of Joy,** Alice Walker, (1992). In this novel about female genital mutilation, the main character uses her anger to deduce meaning and understanding from the procedure she endured.

★ **Possession: A Romance,** A.S. Byatt, (1990). A novel of mystery and love as two young scholars research the lives of two Victorian poets. Booker Prize 1990.

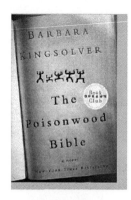

Potiki, Patricia Grace (1995). A Maori community in New Zealand tries to live the old ways and must stand up to developers who want its land. Award-winning novel by one of New Zealand's most decorated writers.

Prism of the Night: A Biography of Anne Rice, Katherine Ramsland, (1991). A companion work for the serious Anne Rice reader.

★ **Prodigal Summer,** Barbara Kingsolver (2000). Three intertwining stories tell of the need to protect and preserve nature and all living things.

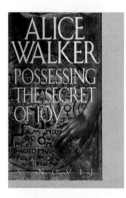

Pure Lust: Elemental Feminist Philosophy, Mary Daly, (1984). Feminist philosopher Daly explores and analyzes a double-sided meaning of lust.

Push, Sapphire, (1996). At 16, Precious is illiterate, constantly abused, and pregnant with a second child. This story tells how she learns to writes about her life and claim it for herself.

Rachel Calof's Story: Jewish Homesteader on the Northern Plains, Rachel Calof, (1995). Recently discovered memoir of a Russian Jewish immigrant's harsh life on the North Dakota prairie at the turn of the century.

Rachel Carson: Witness for Nature, Linda Lear, (1997). An almost 500-page biography, including 120 pages of notes, of writer/scientist Carson who challenged how we care for the planet we live on.

Raising the Stones, Sheri Tepper, (1990). Tepper's novel looks into the future and predicts humanity will survive.

★ **Red Azalea,** Anchee Min, (1994). Facing constant scrutiny, Min's true-life tale of growing up in China during the Cultural Revolution reveals how even the government cannot squelch love and life.

Red China Blues: My Long March from Mao to Now, Jan Wong, (1996), Journalist Wong, a Canadian of Chinese descent, writes of her belief in Mao as she enrolls in Beijing University in 1972, of her education in Canada and the United States as she becomes a correspondent for the New York Times, of her eyewitness view of the Tiananmen Square confrontation and finally of her understanding of the changes in China as well as herself during the past 30 years.

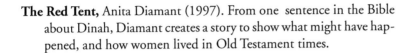

The Red Tent, Anita Diamant (1997). From one sentence in the Bible about Dinah, Diamant creates a story to show what might have happened, and how women lived in Old Testament times.

★ **Refuge: An Unnatural History of Family and Place,** Terry Tempest Williams, (1991). Poet and naturalist Williams weaves reflections about the acts of nature and the dying of her mother.

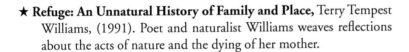

Re-Inventing Eve: Modern Woman in Search of Herself, Kim Chernin, (1988). When Eve is seen as a heroine of "disobedience," her story becomes a transformative vision of woman's place in nature.

Revelations: Diaries of Women, Mary Jane Moffat and Charlotte Painter, eds., (1974). Selections from 32 women's diaries on love, work and power across the centuries.

Revolution From Within: A Book of Self-Esteem, Gloria Steinem, (1992). At the end of her fifth decade, Steinem writes, "It's never too late for a happy childhood."

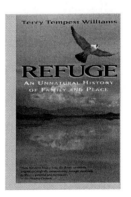

Rift, Lisa Cody, (1988). Africa's Rift valley was irresistible but traveler Fay begins to realize she may never get out.

★ **Riverwalking: Reflections on Moving Water,** Kathleen Dean Moore (1995). In these essays, Moore describes her encounters with the world of rivers and in the process explores philosophical questions about motherhood, happiness, love and loss.

★ **The Road From Coorain,** Jill Ker Conway, (1989). The first female president of Smith College writes of her girlhood in the Australian outback.

The Robber Bride, Margaret Atwood, (1993). Three women, part of each other's lives since the 1960s, are traumatized when three decades later a fourth woman re-enters their lives.

A Romantic Education, Patricia Hampl, (1981). Author's coming of age in Minnesota and her journey to Prague as she explores her family's past.

A Room of One's Own, Virginia Woolf, (1929). Woolf's classic essay, which insists that a woman must have her own money and privacy.

Roseanne: My Life as a Woman, Roseanne Barr, (1989). Roseanne Barr's memoir, from growing up as a Jewish outsider in Salt Lake City through the creation of her TV series.

Sacred Pleasure, Riane Eisler, (1995). Eisler expands her partnership model to envision a society where pleasure,not pain, is the central theme of our lives.

★ **The Samurai's Garden,** Gail Tsukiyama, (1994). The Japanese invasion of China in 1930 is the backdrop for this gentle story of a young 20-year-old Chinese painter who is sent to his grandfather's house in Japan to regain his health.

The Sea, The Sea, Iris Murdoch, (1978). An aging theater director searchs for simplicity and solitude in a lonely house by the North Sea. Booker Prize, 1978.

The Search for Signs of Intelligent Life in the Universe, Jane Wagner, (1986). A hit one-woman play written for Lily Tomlin focuses on the female experience in society.

The Secret Garden, Frances Hodgson Burnett, (1911). Orphaned Mary Lennox is sent to a desolate English mansion where she discovers friendship, love and a hidden garden.

Selected Poems: 1965-1975, Margaret Atwood, (1987). One of the many poetry books of Canadian author Margaret Atwood.

Shape of Red: Insider-Outsider Reflections, Ruth Hubbard and Margaret Randall, (1988). Correspondence between two politically and socially active women who offer radical insights with hopeful vision.

She Walks These Hills, Sharyn McCrumb (1994). Mystery writer and folklorist McCrumb combines the present and past with a 200-year-old ghost story in the Appalachian mountains.

★ **The Ship that Sailed into the Living Room: Sex and Intimacy Reconsidered,** Sonia Johnson, (1991). Johnson challenges the meaning of relationships.

The Shipping News, E. Annie Proulx, (1993). Story of a third-rate newspaperman who retreats to his ancestral home on the Newfoundland coast. Pulitzer Prize 1994, National Book Award 1993.

The Short History of a Prince, Jane Hamilton, (1998). A family story set in Wisconsin centered around a young boy's desire to dance and the challenges he faces growing up as he realizes he is gay.

★ **Silences,** Tillie Olsen, (1965). Olsen explores the social forces that silence the voices of female artists.

Silent Spring, Rachel Carson, (1962). With this book Carson altered the course of history through her concern for the future of the planet.

The Silver DeSoto, Patty Lou Floyd, (1987). Coming-of-age story during the Dust Bowl years in Oklahoma.

Simone de Beauvoir: A Biography, Deirdre Bair, (1990). Based on five years of interviews with the French philosopher, essayist and novelist.

Singer From the Sea, Sheri Tepper (1999). Set in the future on a planet called Haven where the inhabitants all are female, the novel poses questions about technology, religion, treason and love.

Sister Light, Sister Dark, Jane Yolen, (1988). A coming-of-age story based on folklore but set in the future.

Sister Outsider: Essays & Speeches, Audre Lorde, (1984). From her black lesbian feminist perspective, Lorde expands and enriches our understanding of what feminism can be.

The Skeptical Feminist: Discovering the Virgin, Mother, Crone, Barbara Walker, (1987). Walker's spiritual autobiography follows her journey away from Christianity to the three aspects of the Goddess—Virgin, Mother and Crone.

Small Wonder, Barbara Kingsolver, (2002). Essays that explore hope and peace, written in response to September 11.

★ **Solar Storms,** Linda Hogan, (1995). A disturbed young woman returns to her roots in the Boundary Waters between Canada and Minnesota, to learn her history and heal herself.

The Song and the Truth, Helga Ruebsamen, (1997). Lyrical and mysterious tale of a child's paradise lost, set in Java and the Netherlands as World War II encroaches. Translated from the Dutch.

The Song of the Lark, Willa Cather (1915). Considered Cather's most autobiographical novel, "Song" tells of Thea Kronborg's struggle to find her artistic place. As Thea becomes a famous opera singer, she learns that the expected social role for women and the reality of the artistic life are quite different.

Spending: A Utopian Divertimento, Mary Gordon, (1998). As a woman artist turns 50 a whole new world opens for her when a man becomes her muse.

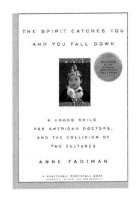

★ **The Spirit Catches You and You Fall Down,** Anne Fadiman, (1997). True story of a Hmong child, her American doctors, and the collision of two cultures. National Book Critics Circle Award 1997.

★ **Spoonhandle,** Ruth Moore, (1946). A bestseller when first published, this novel tells about the Stilwell family, inhabitants of a Maine island, in whom the struggle between love and meanness of spirit, between human dignity and greed is clearly drawn.

The Stone Angel, Margaret Laurence, (1964). Canadian Laurence's novel creates a proud, energetic woman who struggles to hold on to self.

The Stone Diaries, Carol Shields, (1993). Shields chronicles the life of a woman from her birth in 1905 to her death in the mid-'80s. A novel of a woman in search of herself. Pulitzer Prize 1995.

Stones From the River, Ursula Hegi, (1994). Story set in a small town in Germany between 1915 and 1949, told through the eyes of a woman who is a "zwerg"—a dwarf.

The Stories We Hold Secret: Tales of Women's Spiritual Develop-ment, Carol Bruchac, Linda Hogan and Judith McDaniels, eds., (1986). The sacred and hidden stories of 31 women attempting to name experiences with different words.

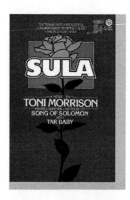

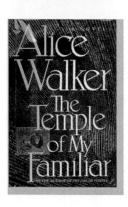

Strength to Your Sword Arm: Selected Writings, Brenda Ueland, (1993). A collection of articles from the Minneapolis author's last four decades.

★ **Sula,** Toni Morrison, (1973). This novel traces the lives of two black women growing up together in Ohio, one choosing to stay and one escaping; both suffering as a result of their choices.

Summer People, Marge Piercy, (1989). A 10-year menage a trois changes one summer because of the presence of the "summer people."

Surfacing, Margaret Atwood, (1972). In this first novel a talented artist, with three companions, journeys to her island growing-up place. While there, the unnamed narrator finds an inner strength to go on with her life.

Surpassing the Love of Men: Romantic Friendship and Love Between Women From the Renaissance to the Present, Lillian Faderman, (1981). Scholarly exploration of the cultural history of women's passionate friendships with each other.

Swimming in the Congo, Margaret Meyers, (1995). Seven-year-old Grace, daughter of missionaries, comes of age in an African landscape, surrounded by both indigenous and foreign people who populate it.

★ **Tales of Burning Love,** Louise Erdrich, (1996). Set in North Dakota, this story intertwines the lives of characters from Erdrich's earlier novels. Four of Jack Mauser's five wives are trapped in a car in a blizzard and recall what it was like to be a wife of Jack.

Talking to High Monks in the Snow: An Asian-American Odyssey, Lydia Minatoya, (1992). Minatoya's memoir of growing up bicultural and her search from her New England roots to her Japanese heritage.

Teaching a Stone To Talk: Expeditions and Encounters, Annie Dillard, (1982). A collection of meditations honoring the natural world.

★ **The Temple of My Familiar,** Alice Walker, (1989). A complex novel with multiple themes, subjects and characters.

Their Eyes Were Watching God, Zora Neale Hurston (1937). This second novel—reprinted in 1978 after heroic efforts by Alice Walker—is the most acclaimed book by folklorist, novelist and anthropologist Hurston. Protagonist Janie, whose love for Tea Cake changes her life, tells her friend Phoeby, "Two things everybody's got to do fuh theyselves. They got tuh go tuh God, and they got tuh find out about livin' fuh theyselves."

★ **These Is My Words: The Diary of Sarah Agnes Prine 1881-1901, Arizona Territories: A Novel,** Nancy Turner, (1998). Turner's novel about a woman's life in southern Arizona in the late 1800s was based on bits of her own family background. Historically and geographically accurate, it celebrates the strength of women in settling the West.

★ **36 Views of Mount Fuji,** Cathy Davidson, (1993). American Davidson teaches at a women's university in Japan. Images of Japanese culture and identity.

Three Times Table, Sara Maitland, (1990). Three generations of women, the grandmother a paleotologist, the daughter a gardener and once-promising mathematician, the granddaughter just leaving childhood.

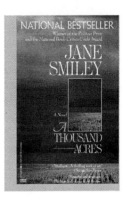

★ **A Thousand Acres,** Jane Smiley, (1991). Modern King Lear story, told through the eyes of three sisters as a father gives up ownership of his thousand acres of Iowa farmland. Pulitzer Prize 1992.

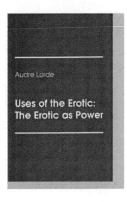

Audre Lorde

Uses of the Erotic:
The Erotic as Power

Through the Burning Steppe: A Memoir of Wartime Russia, 1942-1943, Elena Kohzina (2001). Lyrical and moving memoir of a family's escape from besieged Leningrad to life as city strangers in a Cossack village. A daughter's tribute to her mother.

To Be Real: Telling the Truth and Changing the Face of Feminism, edited by Rebecca Walker (1995). Anthology of essays by young feminists who explore different perspectives regarding the objectives and philosophy of contemporary (Third Wave) feminist theory.

Transforming a Rape Culture, Emilie Buchwald, Pamela Fletcher and Martha Roth, eds., (1993). Writings by women and men of a possible future without rape.

The Travelling Hornplayer, Barbara Trapido (2000). In a bleak twist of fate, the accidental death of a teenage schoolgirl brings together a group of people in London, Cambridge and Edinburgh whose lives intertwine with tragic results.

Two Old Women: An Alaska Legend of Betrayal, Courage and Survival, Velma Wallis, (1993), HarperPerennial, and **Bird Girl and the Man Who Followed the Sun: An Athabascan Legend from Alaska,** Velma Wallis, (1997). Two retellings of ancient legends by Native writer Wallis. Both feature female heroes who face great odds and must find ways to balance their hard-won sense of independence with the traditions of community.

Under the Beetle's Cellar, Mary Willis Walker (1995). Texas journalist Molly Cates is faced with the toughest of assignments as she covers a story of a missing school bus filled with young children.

Unholy Alliances: New Fiction by Women, Louise Rafkin, ed., (1988). Stories from the '80s about relationships just a bit off center.

An Unknown Woman: A Journey to Self Discovery, Alice Koller, (1982). Koller's solitary inward journey during a three-month retreat on Nantucket.

★ **Uses of the Erotic: The Erotic as Power,** Audre Lorde, (1978). An affirmation of the importance of claiming one's sense of the erotic as the source of individual power.

Virginia Woolf, Hermione Lee, (1999). This 800-page biography chronicles Woolf's life and the time in which she lived.

Waist-High in the World: A Life Among the Nondisabled, Nancy Mairs, (1996). Mairs' view of the world from her wheelchair, due to multiple sclerosis, challenges the negative perceptions often held by others. Both intellectual and spiritual, her memoir is told with a direct, honest and witty voice.

★ **The Wall,** Marlen Haushofer, translated by Shaun Whiteside, (1962). The day-by-day survival of a woman who seems to be the only survivor left on earth.

A Weave of Women, E.M. Broner, (1978). A poetic novel weaving together a community of women in the old city of Jerusalem.

Weaving the Visions: Patterns in Feminist Spirituality, Judith Plaskow and Carol Christ, eds., (1989). Contributors, including Asian American, Native American and African American women, present a wide range of views about feminist spirituality.

★ **The Wedding,** Dorothy West, (1995). West, active in the Harlem Renaissance, based her novel on the life she has lived on Martha's Vineyard. She writes of the pain and joy of five generations of a black middle-class American family.

The Well, Elizabeth Jolley, (1986). Set in the Australian farmlands, a novel of the connection between two women, one a lonely older woman, the other a young orphan.

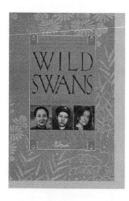

West with the Night, Beryl Markham, (1983). Memoir of an adventurous, independent woman who was raised in colonial Africa in the early part of the century, and became a horse trainer and record-setting aviator. First published in 1942.

What Is Found There: Notebooks in Poetry and Politics, Adrienne Rich, (1993). Rich begins, "This book is about desire and daily life."

White Oleander, Janet Fitch (1999). As a young 12-year-old girl grows up moving from foster home to foster home, she is haunted by the letters her mother writes from jail.

White Teeth, Zadi Smith, (2000). Smith's first novel of two families from Bangladesh and Jamaica who have become part of the melting pot in England. A funny book playing with ideas and language and the tragicomedy of life. Winner of the Whitbread First Novel Award (2000).

★ **Wild Swans: Three Daughters of China,** Jung Chang, (1991). The engrossing story of three generations of Chinese women whose lives spanned feudalism, revolution and cultural revolution (1909-1978).

Wildfire: Igniting the She/Volution, Sonia Johnson, (1989). Johnson presents a feminist anarchy, a woman-created world.

Winter in Taos, Mabel Dodge Luhan, (1935). A simple telling of the daily activities of Mabel Dodge Luhan in her Big House, in the Pueblo and in the village of Taos, New Mexico.

Winter Roads, Summer Fields, Marjorie Dorner, (1992). A collection of stories of families in a Midwestern farm community.

Wisdom of the Heart: Working With Women's Dreams, Karen Signell, (1990). A journey into the world of the female unconscious, based on a feminist perspective.

The Wise Wound: Myths, Realities and Meanings of Menstruation, Penelope Shuttle and Peter Redgrove, (1990). A positive take on a common experience of being woman.

★ **Woman and Nature: The Roaring Inside Her,** Susan Griffin, (1978). Through science, history and imagination, Griffin presents a positive connection between woman and nature.

★ **Woman on the Edge of Time,** Marge Piercy, (1976). A Chicana woman unjustly committed to a mental institution is tuned into the future and heroically helps create a better world.

Woman Warrior: Memoirs of a Girlhood Among Ghosts, Maxine Hong Kingston, (1975). An account of growing up female and Chinese-American in California.

Womanspirit Rising: A Feminist Reader in Religion, Carol Christ, (1979). Introduction to feminist interpretations of religion from 20 women writers.

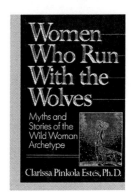

Women and Wilderness, Anne LaBastille, (1980). Wildlife ecologist LaBastille provides history of frontier women as well as 15 case studies of women who currently live in the wilderness.

Women of the Silk, Gail Tsukiyama, (1991). A coming-of-age story in China, set in the 1920s and '30s. Working in the silk factory with other women allows Pei to find strength and independence as the women strike for freedom.

Women, Passion and Celibacy, Sally Cline, (1993). British feminist writer Cline writes of women who have found, in their passion for celibacy, freedom and autonomy to redefine their sexuality.

★ **Women Who Run With the Wolves: Myths and Stories of the Wild Woman Archetype,** Clarissa Pinkola Estés, (1992). Jungian analyst and poet writes about old myths from a new perspective, based on her Latina and Hungarian tradition.

★ **Women's Reality: An Emerging Female System in the White Male Society,** Anne Wilson Schaef, (1981). A book that will let you know you're not sick, bad, crazy or stupid.

★ **Writing a Woman's Life,** Carolyn Heilbrun, (1988). Heilbrun urges women to write of their lives, to name the reality of being woman.

Written on the Body, Jeanette Winterson, (1992). From England, Winterson presents a narrator who has neither name nor gender. Lambda Award 1993.

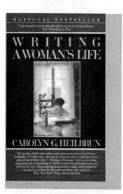

The Yellow Wallpaper, Charlotte Perkins Gilman, (1892). A story of a mental breakdown, based on Gilman's own life.

You Just Don't Understand: Women and Men in Conversation, Deborah Tannen, (1990). Linguistics professor Tannen writes of the complexities of communication between men and women.

★ **Zami: A New Spelling of My Name,** Audre Lorde, (1982). Lorde's "biomythography" of her childhood in Harlem and coming of age in the late '50s.

"GREAT" BECAUSE WE SAY SO!

A brief history of the Great Books of the Western World ("Women need not apply") and the upstart Great Books list from Minnesota Women's Press, Inc., where women set the standard.
By Mollie Hoben.

Ah, the power of naming.

When Glenda Martin decided to expropriate the designation "great book" from the dead white males to whom it traditionally was awarded and apply it instead to books by women, she acted partly with tongue in cheek. But she was also totally serious.

For decades, the Great Books program had been deciding who wrote the most important books of the Western World. And—imagine!— they were all men: Aristotle, Plato, Shakespeare, Milton, Dante, DesCartes, Melville, etc., etc.

Who decided this? Who, in other words, claimed the power of naming greatness? Two men with an agenda.

When Mortimer Adler and Robert Hutchins began to work together in the mid 1940s to promote the Great Books idea, it was a perfect partnership of the academic patriarchy. Both philosopher Adler and educator Hutchins were big fans of Aristotle and St. Thomas Aquinas, and both believed that absolute truths and universal values could be derived from Western classical (i.e., male) thought.

Hutchins had been pushing this idea in the curriculum at the University of Chicago, where he was president, but he believed its real impact would come through adult education.

He started off-campus reading groups, attended at first by members of Chicago's business elite. (Are we safe in assuming they probably were groups of men?) He asked Adler, a philosophy professor at the university, to run the program.

This article first appeared in **BookWomen: A Readers' Community for Those Who Love Women's Words**, October-November, 1996.

The groups caught on, new ones formed, and soon the whole thing got too big for the university to handle. Hutchins and Adler established the Great Books Foundation, and Adler traveled endlessly across the country, speaking and setting up groups, a "Socratic traveling salesman," as one journalist described him.

With Adler's salesmanship and a post-war yearning for what Hutchins called "education for democracy," the idea caught fire. From 167 participants in 1943, it grew to 50,000 readers in 300 cities by 1948. It became something of a fad. The mayor of Chicago proclaimed Great Books Week.

In 1952, the Great Books Foundation published its own editions of the books on the Great Books list—totaling 54 volumes, 32,000 pages, 25 million words. Every word a man's.

If we want to be charitable, we can assume that Adler and Hutchins and their (all-male) panel of experts who helped select entries didn't set out consciously to exclude women. No doubt they didn't consider women writers one way or the other. It was a given, that women's writings did not count when the Big Thinkers were being considered.

This shouldn't be surprising, since the "great" writers they admired operated out of an assumption of women's lesser value.

Consider the two teachers who influenced Adler and Hutchins so deeply. Here's Aristotle, writing in his treatise on "Generation of Animals": "The female is, as it were, a deformed male. The menstrual discharge is semen, though in an impure condition, i.e., it lacks one constituent and one only, the principle of Soul."

Thomas Aquinas, for his part, proposed that, "As God is the principle of the universe, so is man, in likeness to God, the principle of the human race."

By the way, this paraphrase of Aquinas is Susan Griffin's, and I found it, along with the quote from Aristotle, in her classic and profound book, **Woman and Nature: The Roaring Inside Her**.

In that book, Griffin traces the history of patriarchal thinking about women and nature. Interestingly, many of the patriarchs whose misogynistic thinking she analyzes are writers whom Adler and Hutchins deemed "greats." Weaving together their pronouncements, which span the millennia, Griffin shows with chilling effect how these men, and other "great" thinkers, determined these "truths": that women are close to nature, men are above nature, and men's job is to control both women and nature.

I remember the Great Books from my childhood in the '50s. My parents belonged to a group for a while in the Chicago suburb where I grew up. I was impressed by the books themselves—the softbound, im-

In 1952, the Great Books Foundation published its own editions of the books on the Great Books list—totaling 54 volumes, 32,000 pages, 25 million words. Every word a man's.

portant-looking editions, which came in boxed sets—and I believed that if they were called The Great Books, they must be.

When it was my parents' turn to host the group, I would listen to the discussion from my room before falling asleep. I didn't understand much of it, but I was intrigued by the idea of adults as students, actively seeking to learn together through reading and discussion.

So, while my vicarious experience with the Great Books taught me some misleading lessons about who is worthy to read—lessons I had to unlearn later in my life—I also gained a valuable sense of book groups as a good and noble undertaking.

In 1986 (this was before she liberated the term "great books,") Glenda Martin started offering book groups at Minnesota Women's Press, Inc. These groups would read only women's works, she said.

She was not at all apologetic about limiting the reading to women (or, as some skeptics saw it, ignoring men): It was a matter of beginning to right the balance.

The body of women's writings (big, and growing) was new for many readers in Minnesota Women's Press groups, and they were amazed when they discovered so many books by women that touched their hearts, stimulated their thinking, broadened their perspectives, sometimes even changed their lives. At the same time, many were angry that they had never before heard of the books and writers they were discovering.

These reactions sowed the seeds for the Minnesota Women's Press Great Books list. If academics and critics were not going to acknowledge the contributions of women writers, Glenda said, we'd have to do it ourselves!

Thus, every book group at Minnesota Women's Press adds one (or more) titles from its reading to the list. Over the years, groups have selected 301 books by women for designation as Great, and the list keeps growing.

Thus, every book group at Minnesota Women's Press adds one (or more) titles from its reading to the list. Over the years, groups have selected 301 books by women for designation as Great, and the list keeps growing.

Meanwhile, the original Great Books list remained unchanged for 48 years, apparently impervious to growing awareness elsewhere in society about the limitations—not to mention injustice—of looking at anything only through male academic eyes.

Finally, in 1990, the Great Books Foundation added 60 new writers to the canon. Among them were four women: Jane Austen, Willa Cather, George Eliot and Virginia Woolf. The rare great book by a woman does exist, we were told. Four of them, in fact—out of 130.

It could be worse. Not a single writer of color made it to the list. When asked why no African Americans were included, Adler told a reporter for the Nation that it was "because no black American was necessary. No black American has written a great book."

Well, that's settled! No doubt Adler gave similar answers about women when the first list was announced (if anyone thought to ask such a question in the '50s).

In 1990, while Adler and crew grudgingly recognized four female greats, the Great Books list at Minnesota Women's Press contained 36 titles, and that year readers added 20 more, including ones by these greats: Margaret Atwood, Anne Cameron, Rachel Carson, Riane Eisler, Audre Lorde, Gloria Naylor and Marge Piercy.

What makes a book "great"? At Minnesota Women's Press, great books are those books written by women that have most intrigued, fascinated and challenged readers, that provoked strong response and discussion among book group members.

As Glenda says, "These books are great because our readers say they're great!"

GREAT BOOKS FOR CHILDREN OF ALL AGES

Every reader needs her own collection of children's books. In our Reading Retreats and Book Groups on the Road, and in many book groups, we incorporate children's books whenever possible. Here are a few titles that groups have read together and savored. So many wonderful children's books exist these days, this list is just to get you started.

STRONG GIRLS

I Like Me by Nancy Carlson (1988). A charming pig admires her finer points and recalls all the fun she's had being herself.

I'm a Girl! by Lila Jukes, illustrated by Susan Keeter (1995). Affirmations of what it means to be a girl.

Princess Smartypants by Babette Cole (1986). This is one independent princess.

Ruby Mae Has Something To Say by David Small (1992). Ruby Mae speaks for peace.

Rosie and Michael by Judith Viorst, illustrated by Lorna Tomei (1974). Two friends share with each other.

Sheila Rae, the Brave by Kevin Henkes (1987). Two sisters explore being afraid and being brave.

CARING BOYS

I Can Hear the Sun by Patrica Polacco (1996). The orphan Fondo becomes friends with an animal keeper as together they care for a blind goose who lives by the lake.

The Lady in the Box by Ann McGovern, illustrated by Marni Backer (1997). When Ben and Lizzie discover a homeless woman living in their neighborhood, they must reconcile their desire to help with their mother's admonition not to talk to strangers.

Rosie and Michael by Judith Viorst, illustrated by Lorna Tomei (1974). Two friends share with each other.

Tomas and the Library Lady by Pat Mora, illustrated by Raul Colon (1997). Based on the life of a young migrant boy the library lady becomes key as he explores a new place.

Wilfred Gordon McDonald Partridge by Mem Fox, illustrated by Julie Vivas (1985). A boy becomes friends with several elderly folk.

Willie's Not the Hugging Kind by Joyce Durham Barrett, illustrated by Pat Cummings (1989). Willie is convinced by his best friend that hugs are silly, but soon he misses hugs and must find a way to become huggable again.

CONNECTIONS ACROSS CULTURES

Carly by Annegert Fuchshuber (1995). A homeless girls finds place with a fool.

Dinner at Aunt Connie's House by Faith Ringgold (1993). At Aunt Connie's house Melody meets 12 inspiring African-American women, who step out of their portraits and join the family for dinner.

Feathers and Fools by Mem Fox, illustrated by Nicholas Wilton (1996). The peacocks and swans allow fear of their differences to lead to destruction—but a new generation offers hope.

How My Parents Learned To Eat by Ina R. Friedman, illustrated by Allen Say (1984). A girl recalls the story of how her Japanese mother learned to eat with silverware and her American father with chopsticks.

The Serpent Slayer and Other Stories of Strong Women by Katrin Tchana, illustrated by Trina Schart Human (2000). Tales from around the world, in which the main characters are strong and resourceful women.

Street Rhymes Around the World edited by Jane Yolan (1992). Chants and songs sung by children in different nations, with each rhyme illustrated by an artist native to the country.

CONNECTIONS BETWEEN GENERATIONS

A Chair for My Mother by Vera Williams (1982). A daughter, mother and grandmother save dimes to buy a comfortable chair.

Grandmother's Pigeons by Louise Erdrich, illustrated by Jim LaMarche (1996). Passenger pigeons are discovered in Grandmother's bedroom after she departs for Greenland on a porpoise.

How Does It Feel To Be Old? by Norma Farber, illustrated by Trina Hyman (1979). A grandmother tells with warmth and honesty what it means to get old.

Just Us Women by Jeanette Caines, illustrated by Pat Cummings (1982). A girl and her aunt plan a car trip just for the two of them.

The Table Where Rich People Sit by Byrd Baylor, illustrated by Peter Parnall (1994). How much is it worth to live the life you desire, close to nature? A girl's parents help her answer this question.

Wanda's Roses by Pat Brisson, illustrated by Maryann Cocca-Leffler (1994). Wanda nurtures a bare bush in an empty lot and is nurtured by the adults in her neighborhood.

EARTH AND ALL LIVING THINGS

A Story for Bear by Dennis Haseley, illustrated by Jim LaMarche (2002). Even bears like to have stories read to them.

Everybody Needs a Rock by Byrd Baylor, illustrated by Peter Parnnall (1974). Each of us needs a rock for peace and security.

I'm in Charge of Celebrations by Byrd Baylor, illustrated by Peter Parnall (1986). A daily celebration of life in the southwest desert.

Insectlopedia by Douglas Florian (1998). Short, fun poems and illustrations about such insects as the inchworm, termite, cricket and mayfly.

Miss Rumphius by Barbara Cooney (1982). Great-aunt Rumphius wished to make the part of her world more beautiful by planting flowers.

Mole Music by David McPhail (1999). Mole learns to play the violin and his music has a greater effect on others than he will ever know.

The Mushroom Man by Ethel Pochocki, illustrated by Barry Moser (1993). Mushroom man and mole become friends.

JOY OF LAUGHTER

Earrings by Judith Viorst, illustrated by Lola Langner Malone (1993). What's a young girl to do when her parents refuse to let her have her ears pierced?

Elizabeth and Larry by Marilyn Sadler, illustrated by Roger Bollen (1990). Elizabeth's best friend is an alligator.

Hogula: Dread Pig of Night by Jean Gralley (1999). Hogula goes out to find a friend, and one finds him.

Never Fear, Snake My Dear! By Rolf Siegenthaler (1999). A mouse and a snake become friends.

Purple Hair? I Don't Care! By Dianne Young, illustrations by Barbara Hartmann (1994). This is one special baby.

You Read to Me, I'll Read to You by Mary Ann Hoberman, illustrations by Michael Emberley (2001). Poetry to read together.

FOR ALL BOOK LOVERS

The Library by Sarah Stewart, illustrated by David Small (1995). In memory of the real Mary Elizabeth Brown, who loved books.

Library Lil by Suzanne Williams, illustrated by Steven Kellogg (1997). A librarian brings reading to a small town and a television-watching gang, as well.

part two:
GREAT BOOK GROUPS

"I consider book groups boring if there is not a little tension in the discussion, if there are not several diverse views offered."
—Glenda Martin, Book Groups Facilitator

Long before the media "discovered" women's book groups, they were hot at Minnesota Women's Press, Inc. In "Starting a Great Group," Glenda Martin shares insights she's gained over the years of facilitating many different kinds of book groups.

Then we highlight book groups of various kinds, from around the country, each a rich source of ideas and approaches to try for yourself. The descriptions—in the groups' own words—come from our bi-monthly magazine **BookWomen: A Readers' Community for Those Who Love Women's Words.**

We conclude with a list of questions that other readers have found work well to elicit lively book-group discussion.

the great books

STARTING A GREAT GROUP

Advice from 17 years of leading book groups: Procedures may vary but basic principles hold true, and it's the personal exchanges that make the experience rich. By Glenda Martin.

Are you unhappy with your book group? Are individuals disagreeing about the content of the book, taking it personally and going home disgruntled? Do only one or two of the group members do most of the talking, as well as the choosing of the books to be read? Does the discussion never seem to go beneath the surface? If so, you may need to find another group to join, or, better yet, start one of your own.

Perhaps better to start a new one than to have to call in a mediator; I understand some groups now need to do just that.

How to begin? When we were thinking about starting book groups at Minnesota Women's Press, Inc. 17 years ago, I asked eight women to meet with me for a year, once a month, at homes and at our office. Sort of a mini-research project.

They were to help determine what book groups sponsored by the Women's Press might look like. Those eight women did meet and provided many of the guidelines now used for groups at the Women's Press as well as the 10 groups I've created in Arizona.

Book selection is the key factor. It was a given that we would read books written by women, building on the founding principles of Minnesota Women's Press, Inc. that every woman has a story and each individual story is valuable.

We explored a wide variety of possible themes that first year, and we found satisfaction in coming up with books to fit each theme. Over the years since, one of my favorite responsibilities as facilitator has been collecting many different titles for consideration. Then, when groups gather and add their own ideas of possible books, it's a great way to be introduced to a wide range of books and authors.

This article first appeared, in slightly different form, in **BookWomen: A Readers' Community for Those Who Love Women's Words**, June-July, 1999.

In our year together, we also found that selecting books for at least two to four months at a time is helpful for readers and saves taking time from every meeting. My personal preference is that books be chosen for an entire year if the group meets year round.

Since the beginning, two genres have seldom been read for discussion in group's I've facilitated: romance and mystery. These are best-selling genres, and many in our book groups are avid readers of one or both (especially mystery), but typically these two genres do not provide a good opportunity for in-depth discussion.

However, when requests kept surfacing for a mystery group I agreed to facilitate one for two years. Mystery fans loved it. To enhance discussion we read three mysteries a month around a theme and then did a compare/contrast. We also looked briefly at biographical information about each writer and her work.

In addition to book selection, our pilot-project group considered the where, when and how aspects of meeting. The preference was to meet monthly, on weekday evenings, early, for two hours, without food. Also, it became important to meet consistently at one specified location rather than a different site each month.

How many women in a group? We decided that eight members, the size of the pilot group, was the minimum needed. Over the 17 years my guideline has become an enrollment of 15, which means usually there will be anywhere from 8 to 14 in attendance.

After that first year, book groups took off at Minnesota Women's Press. We went on to sponsor hundreds of groups; some were designed to be of limited duration, such as 6-12 sessions, others have gone on for years and years.

Some groups have focused on a genre, such as Biography, Autobiography, Memoir, Letter and Diary (we call it "BAMLAND") or Science Fiction/Fantasy. Some are based on a theme: the Earth group, for example, or the Talking Peace group. Others have a particular approach: the Booker Group reads only prize winners; the Books Afoot group combines reading and hiking.

A group that has met for 15 years began by reading all of May Sarton's work, chronologically, and the members now have read several other authors' entire works, in order, including Louise Erdrich, Toni Morrison, Alice Walker and Barbara Kingsolver. This group calls itself the Reading Across a Lifetime group.

When we started getting into book groups in a big way, they were not yet a common phenomenon. Now, of course, they've proliferated around the country. I've experienced this during my years in southern Arizona. In 1998, 13 women signed up for a book group I offered at the local bookshop in Green Valley. Five years later, I was facilitating 10 groups with 150 women

The key for me is the connection with the variety of thoughtful women readers that book groups offer. It is the personal stories and questions that surface from the books we read that enhance our reading.

participating, ranging from the northern suburbs of Tucson to the southern art community of Tubac.

The majority of these groups meet once a month and continue year after year. A variety of themes have been chosen for year-long focus. For example, "Women Writers Across the USA," "Reading Across the Genres," "Around the World with Women Authors" and "Southwestern Women Writers."

Some groups meet for four to six months, every other week. Recent themes for these sessions have been "Prolific Women Novelists You May Not Have Read," and "All History is Fiction and Personal."

Studying one book or one author in detail is an exciting challenge for a book group. For example, in Arizona, we met once a week for a month to study Native American writer Leslie Marmon Silko's **Almanac of the Dead**. This 750-page novel, set in the Tucson area, took Silko 10 years to write, and it addresses some of the excesses of the human experience.

I'm remembering a group I did in Minnesota where we read all of Silko's work. One participant, a young businesswoman, read the first 50 pages of "Almanac," did not want to continue because it seemed too dark, but finished because the group found it so powerful.

A number of months later she was diagnosed with pancreatic cancer, and over the next several months, as she attended book group she shared the depths of what was happening to her. The last two months of her life the entire group went to her, for she was now too ill to make it to the Women's Press.

The final time we met with her, only three weeks before her death, she told us how important Silko's book had been. We then read together the last pages from her favorite book, **The Mists of Avalon**, by Marion Zimmer Bradley. As Morgaine steps through the mists to Avalon, our young friend said, "Isn't that beautiful?" No greater gift could she have given us than sharing her dying with us.

It is the power of the personal stories that stays with me. No matter how important books and reading are, the key for me is the connection with the variety of thoughtful women readers that book groups offer. It is the personal stories and questions that surface from the books we read that enhance our reading.

Every group begins with a question that relates the content or a theme of the book to personal experience. We go around, not skipping anyone, hearing individual responses to the question. In this way we not only start the discussion right off on a meaningful plane, we also learn about each other's lives. We develop a sense of connection to each person, even though the only time we may see each other is during book-group time. This is part of the effort to build a woman-based, book-loving community. (For some examples, see page 58.)

With each new group, I begin with two statements. One is, "We are not school." No one has to read the book, or be concerned if they read only part of the book; they are welcome to come and listen, to ask questions and perhaps then to decide they will read the book. We are not gathered to provide an academic, analytical critique of the author's intent, but rather to explore the meaning of the book for our own selves.

On the other hand, "We are not therapy," either, even though it is true many of the books we read will bring forth personal experiences. As facilitator, I try to ensure that no one person dominates the discussion and that every person who wishes has an opportunity to speak. But this role is a responsibility I encourage everyone in the group to share.

How satisfying when participants tell me they feel fortunate to have read books they had not previously known about. How affirming when readers have re-read a book for the group and come saying how much richer it became on the second read.

I know the power of re-reading, for I try to re-read a book every time I use it in a group. In fact, if a book does not hold up in a second reading, I do not use that book again.

Book groups seem boring to me if there is not a bit of tension in the discussion, if there are not several diverse views offered. If everyone is in total agreement about a book, I seldom mention it to other groups for potential discussion, though certainly I let others know about books that everyone loves.

Certainly my love of books is a major factor in my life. But it is the people that really hook me in groups. The variety and range of ideas that each brings to a book creates the real excitement. My life is full of wonderful personal stories of the impact of books on women's lives.

For me, book groups are about the people as much as the books. I am enriched by both. If your book group isn't quite working for you, do a little research, organize a bit differently and you'll be amazed at the riches that will be added to your life.

We develop a sense of connection to each person, even though the only time we may see each other is during book group. This is part of the effort to build a woman-based, book-loving community.

Starting out

A question that relates the content of the book to personal experience can be a powerful way to start book group discussion. Here are some examples of questions I've used in groups.—Glenda Martin

Breaking Clean by Judy Blunt. Montana ranch woman Judy Blunt takes her three children, leaves her husband and moves to town when it becomes clear she will never inherit any of the land she loves.
Can you imagine anything in your life that would cause you to take such a bold, drastic step in order to create your own life?

Cactus Thorn by Mary Austin. Austin has written a story that parallels her own experience. She is immersed in the connection of women and the land, the way women take care of it and the way it teaches and heals them.
How do you respond to this concept of connection?

Gone to Soldiers by Marge Piercy. This novel of World War II revolves around the lives of 10 women and men.
Which of the roles they played during the war was new to you?

The Master Butcher's Singing Club by Louise Erdrich. Erdrich shows us a strong friendship between the butcher's wife, Eva, and the unusual Delphine Watzka.
Have you had a strong friendship with a woman similar to this?

Moon Tiger by Penelope Lively. Claudia is dying and she is composing in her head the history of her life. She wonders whether a "kaleidoscopic view might be an interesting heresy."
What kaleidoscopic view would you present of history in your life?

Pavilion of Women by Pearl Buck. The main character, Madame Wu, changes her life at 40.
What was your life like when you were 40? Or, if you are not yet that age, what does turning 40 mean to you?"

GROWING A GREAT GROUP

Reading is a solitary activity, yet most book women yearn to share. They love to talk about a good book with others who've also read it; they relish the give and take of discussion around books. That's why reading groups fill a need in so many book women's lives.

At our magazine, BookWomen, we hear regularly from readers about their book groups. One fact stands out: no two reading groups are alike. They organize and focus their gatherings in many different and creative ways. Here's a sampling of ideas and inspiration from groups from around the country.

SOLITARY READERS JOIN FORCES

Like generations of women before them, these avid readers find pleasure and enrichment in each other's company.

In 1989, two friends and I began to muse about reading, about how much time we individually spent hunched over our books. We also spoke about how solitary an act reading was. What could we do to make it more meaningful, we wondered, more communal, a shared activity. Hello? ... Book Club!

We were aware that for hundreds of years before us, women had gathered together for many reasons—sewing, quilting, cooking AND reading, mostly for the pleasure of each others' company. But our idea still seemed new to us.

So, with excitement and a little nervousness, we gathered up a few of our reading friends, had our first meeting and discovered that we were indeed a unique group of "Women Who Read Too Much." But we read a lot of the wrong stuff. We wanted to add more quality and substance to our reading experience, and thought a book club would put pressure on us to finish all those books we "meant to read" but didn't.

We choose a discussion leader for each meeting who is also expected to look up material on the author. When the discussion begins, we stay with it until we feel we have covered the material sufficiently and everyone has had her say.

Women Who Read Too Much
Oshkosh, Wis.

Started: 1989

Ages: 40s-70s

What makes it work:
"Our affection and respect for each other, plus our very wacky collective sense of humor, are some of the things that keep us together."

We are not afraid to speak out, but we do respect each other's opinions and are careful not to tread on each other's sensibilities. Our conversations are informal and easygoing, and fluctuate from quiet and thoughtful moments to wild and chaotically funny observations about our reading material.

We choose three books at a time, preferring not to define our coming year with planning too far ahead. We try hard to be adventurous in our book selecting and prefer not to be locked in or limited to too many typical book-club choices, although we do read many of the same books that everyone else is reading, for good reason.

In addition to books, we all love movies and keep adding to our video list. We also enjoy our "poetry nights," where we read our favorite poems to each other.

I send out a newsletter every two or three months, containing information about choices and locations of meetings. Each issue also contains a "review" of our last meeting: comments and quotes from our recently discussed book. I include a list of books our members have mentioned that will not necessarily be chosen for discussion but are interesting reads.

Sigrid Nunez, in her first and prize-winning novel, **A Feather on the Breath of God**, perfectly describes an aspect of our group's reading experience: "I had discovered the miraculous possibility that art holds out to us; to be a part of the world and to be removed from the world at the same time."—**Jane MacAndrew**, Oshkosh, Wis.

From an article in **BookWomen**, Dec. 1999-Jan. 2000

DEMOCRACY IN ACTION

Selecting books for a year takes a lot of energy. Decadent deserts help the process.

Read and Feed Book Group
Albuquerque, N.M.

Started: 1978

Members: "We are married, single, divorced; with young children, grown children, no children. As would be expected, we have seen births, deaths, divorces, marriages, changed careers, etc."

Once a year, at a very raucous and sometimes contentious afternoon potluck, we choose our books for the next 11 months. Sometimes we go with a theme (e.g., international writers) and other years we don't. Recently, after reading some "highly recommended" books that we all hated, we initiated the policy that the person recommending the book must have read it first.

Everybody comes prepared to discuss the books she is proposing; we write the names of the books on a large easel, and everyone votes for 11 books. One of the books must be a classic (a somewhat elastic category) and the books must be available in the library—which means that, as a group, we don't read "best sellers."

The 11 books with most votes win. The other books go on our "also recommended list." When we select books, we also select the house and the date of the monthly meeting. After the meeting, one of our members enters everything onto her computer and publishes a book list for that year, complete with meeting dates, hostess names and alternate books.

Sometime after that, our librarian member (a web master) enters the information onto our web site, www.unm.edu/~ccrowley/bookclub. She also updates the site periodically and passes on group-related information such as the availability of that month's book through interlibrary loan, etc.

We've found that the books we all enjoyed are not necessarily the best ones for discussion. It is the books not all of us have liked that have gotten us the most agitated.

We call ourselves Read 'n Feed, and we try to get all of our socializing done while we are eating our dessert in the beginning of the meeting. As for our desserts, we are not talking Twinkies. Our treats are generally homemade and we tend to go all out. When we were younger, we were heavily into decadent chocolate desserts; now, while still decadent, the desserts are a bit more varied. When we can, we try to have the dessert fit the book that we have just finished reading.—**Nan Burke**, Albuquerque, N.M.

From an article in **BookWomen**, Aug.-Sept., 1999

THE TIES THAT BIND
Through reading and sharing, these women develop bonds that enrich their lives.

Our book group's name—WD40—stands for Women's Discussion Over 40, an undertaking that lubricates our minds and spirits.

Over the years it has been exciting to witness what one charter member experienced as "opening a whole new world of literature." Participating in WD40 even expanded what she read outside the group, she said. Another member, a history buff and self-described "political junkie," said that reading literature was new to her.

We have read mostly fiction by women authors, but approximately a fourth of our books were written by men and another quarter were non-fiction. Toni Morrison and Barbara Kingsolver are our favorite authors, hands down.

Books informing us of different cultures, both within this country and throughout the world—and particularly women's experiences within those cultures—have been very appealing.

WD40 Book Group
Carlsbad, Calif.

Special traditions:
"Our annual December potluck supper is a favorite time to 'party' together, sharing food and wine. Overnight retreats at a nearby Benedictine abbey have given us a chance for special bonding as well as more time to look at and choose future books."

Our discussions are richer now than when we began because we've built a repertoire of reading history. Frequently we find ourselves referring back to a previous book's event or theme, making comparisons.

The monthly meeting of WD40 has become a special time for all of us, when we not only discuss books, but also share and support each other's ups and downs, joys and sorrows. It is a safe place! Above all, WD40 is a wonderful group of women who now have a remarkable history together.

One thing I have learned is that women need women—for sharing and caring, for understanding and growing. Unlike the women in **The Red Tent**, we face separation from our mothers, aunts and daughters in an ever more complex, confusing, changing world. We yearn for nurturing relationships with other women.

A book group can help to provide this missing link in modern society. For me, WD40 provides some of this connection.—**Mary Ellen Gregg**, Carlsbad, Calif.

From an article in **BookWomen**, June-July, 2001

MY MOTHER'S BOOK CLUB

How 26 women with no money for books and no library made sure they had novels to read all year.

Rural Book Club
Iowa, 1930s

Favorite authors of the group included:
Bess Streeter Aldrich
Emilie Loring
Temple Bailey
Gene Stratton Porter.

It was the 1930s, a time of depression when money was scarce on the farms of southern Iowa where I grew up. My mother was an avid reader, but she couldn't afford to buy books and there was no library in the community.

In order to be able to read new books, she and 25 other housewives started a Book Club. Once a year someone secured a list of new novels just published, and the women met and each selected a book to order. Each woman bought one book a year and got to read 26.

The books were passed to another, usually the closest neighbor, every two weeks. Book Club was also a main social event for the women. Each woman paired with another and hosted the group one month of the year. This was a time to catch up with each other's lives as well as to talk about books.—**Lois Garrett**, Two Harbors, Minn.

From an article in **BookWomen**, Dec. 1999-Jan. 2000

MOTHERS AND DAUGHTERS READ TOGETHER

What happens when mothers and their pre-teen daughters get together to talk books?

Nine mothers and their daughters gathered one recent Sunday evening at our home to enjoy each other's company and eat a dinner of "prairie fare" (savory meat pie, pureed butternut squash, and berry crisp a la mode). Oh, yes, and to discuss **Sarah, Plain and Tall** by Patricia MacLachlan, the book we selected to launch our Mother-Daughter Book Club.

Most of us had never been in a book club, let alone one that crossed generations the way this one does. Bolstered with organizing tips from **The Mother-Daughter Book Club** by Shireen Dodson, we knew we couldn't go too far wrong. Moreover, I felt inspired about the purpose of the club: to use books as a vehicle for moms and their daughters to talk about real life issues together.

"Sarah, Plain and Tall" was a great way to begin. It took about an hour to read. We heard some delightful stories of how the teams worked together: moms read to daughters; daughters read to mothers; some read separately. In all cases, the book became a topic of conversation before the meeting.

My daughter Casey and I prepared discussion questions ahead of time, with the goal of using the book to think about our own lives. Before we got to the book, however, we asked each mother-and-daughter pair to introduce each other. It was wonderful to hear the pride expressed by the moms and the daughters' descriptions of their mothers.

For each meeting, a mother-daughter pair will select a book and host a gathering. In our case, my daughter and I really shared the workload, too. Casey helped get the invitations out, consulted on the menu, arranged the flowers and candles, peeled apples and peaches, and typed up the membership list and monthly sign-up sheet. She didn't help with the cleanup, but that will come in time! (Anybody know of a book that will bring that lesson home?)—**Laureen Andrews**, Washington, D.C.

From an article in **BookWomen**, Dec. 1999-Jan. 2000

Mother-Daugher Book Group
Washington, D.C.

How to start a mother-daughter group: "Ask a friend or two with daughters what they think, plant the idea with a larger group (bill it as a kind of party with good food and lots of conversation), then take the plunge—set a date, select a book, plan a menu and prepare for discussion. You will not regret it!"

GROUP GETS REAL ABOUT FEMINISMS

**Augsburg College
Book Group**
Minneapolis, Minn.

The challenge:
"Too often on a college
campus a reading
group like this stays too
academic; participants
tend to keep a distance
perhaps appropriate
for the classroom. Our
challenge was to
sustain discussions,
across generations,
in an informal
atmosphere."

This group formed to read one book and existed for only a month, but it forged meaningful connections and made a difference for participants.

Armed with **To Be Real**, an anthology about third-wave feminism edited by Rebecca Walker, 25 women at Augsburg College, Minneapolis, Minn., set out to explore this question: "Is feminism dead?" We were professors, students and staff of different ages and of divergent backgrounds, positions and experiences.

We met once a week for a month, discussing the essays in Walker's book and the issues they raised. We spent a lot of time talking about the past—where we had been, what we believed feminism to be, what we thought of the progression of feminism over the last few decades.

We all had different definitions of what feminism is (or is not). That is, we all had personal feminisms and they sometimes contradicted each other. Our discussions were not always easy or comfortable.

This is precisely, though, what "To Be Real" is all about. The writers in this anthology set out to reclaim contradictions as inherent to any movement like feminism that seeks diverse outlooks and teaches autonomous thought.

At times, the essays caused some real tension in the group. Most of the articles do not attempt to answer or settle the problems they address. We in the reading group used the book more as a jumping-off point for animated discussion and further reading than as a source of solutions.

While there were generational differences in the group, I was surprised to find how much the same issues were important to women no matter what their age.—**C. J. Mace**, Minneapolis, Minn.

From an article in **BookWomen**, June-July, 2000

READING WITH A PURPOSE

Variety is the spice of (reading) life for this group.

The group's philosophy for book discussion echoes that of Paule Marshall in **Praisesong for the Widow**: "You become involved and you think, because there is a good story and the story needs to be told." She describes women's gatherings as "a form of inexpensive therapy and an outlet for their enormous creative energy."

We choose selections for the year by consensus, and the list usually includes contemporary fiction, a classic, non-fiction, a play and poetry—primarily by women. During the holiday season, we have included our favorite children's stories, and one year in May we each brought our favorite cookbook, along with samples, for a potluck.

Members volunteer to be discussion leaders and add much color to their presentations. One member who frequently visits New Mexico led the discussion for **Death Comes for the Archbishop** by Willa Cather. She displayed a large map of the area, along with photographs and many artifacts of the Southwest.

Reading plays offers not only good discussion but also the opportunity to become actors, as we take roles and read parts of the play aloud. We try to choose a play that one of our local small theaters is going to produce. Then we can attend it together, and often the director and actors agree to meet and discuss the play with us after the curtain comes down. Poetry discussions have included guests from the local poets groups.

We are "Reading with a Purpose" to foster our own interests in literature, theater and poetry, and to share and enrich our collective understanding of books, ourselves and one another.— **Elaine Schmidt and Laurie Dean** (mother and daughter), Rochester, Minn.

From an article in **BookWomen**, April-May, 1997

Reading with a Purpose Book Group
Rochester, Minn.

Affiliation: one of three AAUW book groups in Rochester

Began: 1975

Where book ideas come from: Book-Women, other AAUW groups, individual members, national book groups.

THE LITERARY WORKPLACE

Lock the doors, Put the "Closed" sing in the window. It's staff book group time.

Many companies provide pension plans and medical insurance for their employees as well as paid sick days and vacation time. An extra benefit Minnesota Women's Press, Inc. offers its employees is our monthly staff book discussion group.

Those who choose to participate gather in the conference room with brown bag lunches the second Tuesday of every month to enjoy an hour and a half of energetic, stimulating discussion. We read fiction, non-fiction, science fiction and essays, eager for new ways to view our world, understand relationships and bring insights to our thinking.

Munching our apples and carrot sticks, we debate and discuss the books, weaving in our own beliefs and experiences. A bond has grown between group members as we express different opinions, and we expand our understanding as we listen to different viewpoints.

The group began in 1993, in order to read and discuss the just-published anthology, **Transforming a Rape Culture**, edited by Emilie Buchwald, Pamela Fletcher and Martha Roth. Our goal was to study the problem of sexual violence in our culture. We met for nine weeks, and

Minnesota Women's Press Staff Book Group
St. Paul, Minn.

Why it's important: "We discover dimensions of each other that we may not have a chance to notice otherwise in the busy-ness of work."

our discussions were intense and passionate as we explored ways to change fundamental attitudes and ideas that create a rape culture.

Wanting to continue reading together, we switched to a monthly schedule. Some of our most provocative discussions have been about books several of us will say we didn't like. Sometimes we rail at the hero/protagonist in a book, wanting her to make different decisions or wiser choices.

One staff person said about the book group, "Now we can plan our vacations around our favorite books." On the other hand, some of us have been known to come in from vacation to attend book group. That's the way it is when you like your company and the company in your book group.—**Carol Schuldt**, St. Paul, Minn.

From an article in **BookWomen**, June-July, 1997

TEACHERS READ (TOO)

These teachers discover that a book group creates a stimulating forum for professional development.

Current issues in education have been the focus of this particular book club. We have read a variety of books exploring topics chosen by the teachers, such as gender and identity, multicultural and multilingual classrooms, competition in educational settings, homosexuality and adolescence, and middle-grade needs.

Our book club takes a dynamic and teacher-friendly approach: In lieu of the more academic and cumbersome research articles proffered by the educational elite, we read novels and popular nonfiction based on current research.

Questions are raised about how we handle our daily practices, and this leads to candid discussions about concerns, fears and successes in the classroom and in the research field. As may be expected, we raise more questions than provide answers, but the opportunity to discuss and reflect with peers is a precious commodity in our schools, which this book club can provide.

Since we started, the role of the book and the role of the teacher have evolved. At first, the book of choice was our main focus, and delving into the layers of the topic at hand was primary. But, over the course of this whole process, "the book" has become a starting point for inquiry into the culture of the teachers' own middle school. Teachers have expanded their definition of themselves from "group participant" to "teacher researcher" as the books have pressed their buttons and touched their hearts.

Certainly, the impact of this professional-development book club reaches beyond the group participants. Participating teachers have commented that they find themselves discussing the books and topics with other teachers and with their students. It's a wonderful opportunity for teachers to model the process of life-long learning and inquiry.

Although there were concerns initially that a book club as a form of professional development would not be fruitful or "professional," the teachers have shown, year after year, that reading books that illuminate educational and social issues does have an impact on personal reflection and classroom practices. The book club has given our educational community an opportunity to re-examine what it means to grow professionally and improve instructional practice.—**Laura Brader-Araje**, Chapel Hill, N.C.

From an article in **BookWomen**, June-July, 2000

MY VIRTUAL BOOK GROUP

Neither snow nor sleet nor below-zero temperatures keep these readers from connecting around books.

I wanted a book group. But time, location and circumstance seemed to conspire against it. That didn't stop me from reading, of course.

One day a friend handed me a mystery she had just read and liked. I read it and passed it on. Soon mysteries were making the rounds of a select group of friends. On the inside cover we'd write our names, often with notations: "only read 1/3" or "can't stand the characters." In addition to input from previous readers, the entries also afforded us a quick reminder if we'd already read the book, which if we had to check was a pretty good critique of the story.

Books were packaged and sent on to friends out of town, and the sharing continued. The fax would come alive with lists of must-reads, comments on authors or books to avoid like yellow snow. The mystery circle expanded. My Anchorage friend and I began to include more "literary" tomes and books we'd heard about by women authors. We devoured them and discussed them via mail and weekly phone calls.

We've been doing this for years, undirected and spontaneous. This is my book club, our individual meeting place where no one has to vacuum, get dressed or clean in preparation for the meetings.

We meet our needs, read and discuss our books and grow in our friendships. Not much more could be expected from the most organized

Non-group Book Group
Alaska

Why it works: "Nothing more could be accomplished if we were all in a room together, which can be difficult, considering our distances, the snow and normal winter temperatures of –20. We've overcome the challenges of schedules, babies, husbands, and weather."

of book clubs. As a noted philosopher of my time, Mick Jagger, says, "You can't always get what you want, but if you try, sometimes, you get what you need."—**Michel Landeman**, North Pole, Alaska

From an article in **BookWomen**, Feb.-March, 1997

SHORT BUT SWEET

Reading short stories can take book group discussion to new depths.

Classic Short Story Book Group
West Lafayette, Ind.

Started: 1975, an interest group of the Purdue University Women's Club

What they read:
"Over the years, the group has read a wide range of short-story collections, mainly 20th-century literature written by American, Canadian, English and a variety of international authors."

In the Classic Short Story Group of West Lafayette, Ind., members meet twice a month for two hours with two short stories as assigned reading for each session. Allotting a full hour for a lively and informed in-depth discussion of each short story gives time to question everything from the meaning of the title to an interpretation of the last words, and everything in between. Everyone can literally be on the same page and puzzle together over words and phrases. Close reading teases out nuances of character, plot and theme.

One member fondly sees it as a wonderful group "synergy" that results from sharing different viewpoints and interpretations. And the necessary economy and intensity of a short story often delivers a powerful emotional punch that may be more diffuse in a novel.

As women's lives have become busier, members can still find time to read four short stories in a month when perhaps they could not read an entire novel. Research on authors and stories also is easier in the Internet age.

Another plus of reading short stories is the convenience and economy of buying copies of only one book for an entire year or more. Reading short stories exposes the group to the work of authors who do not write novels. Members sometimes discover a fascinating story by a writer they had never heard of, with research revealing an impressive life and literary career in her or his lifetime. On the other hand, several well-known women novelists have written short stories that are interesting to compare and discuss.

Whatever the story, the group agrees that the fun and reward of reading it is talking it over together at leisure. —**Nancy Hagen Patchen**, West Lafayette, Ind.

From an article in **BookWomen**, April-May, 2003

READING ACROSS A LIFETIME

Reading all the books of one author, in the order she wrote them, can be a powerful and moving experience.

Reading Across a Lifetime Book Group
St. Paul, Minn.

Started: 1991

Spin off: "Members came to feel such a connection to this woman that often they would ask, 'When are we going to Maine to visit May Sarton?' It was this query that got us thinking about taking book groups on the road, and in 1997 we offered a Book Group on the Road to Maine."

It began with the writings of May Sarton. None of us could have predicated the rich learning and experiences we would have over the next years. The most important thing we learned in this book group was the depth with which a reader comes to know an author through reading the entire body of her work chronologically.

This happened to us as we read, in the order she wrote them, all of Sarton's 49 published books. Over the years that this reading took, we came to know Sarton at all the stages of her writing career; as the young poet, the mid-life memoirist and novelist, the writer in her 80s publishing her last book.

Then there was no more Sarton work to explore. What could the group do next? We enjoyed friendship and discussion with each other, we had learned how powerful it was to read an author chronologically and we wanted to continue to connect our reading to an admired author.

Ah, what better way that to read authors Sarton had mentioned in her memoirs—all their works, chronologically. So it was decided, and the group became known as the Reading Across a Lifetime book group. Some of the authors whose works we have since read chronologically include Barbara Kingsolver, Louise Erdrich, Toni Morrisson, Doris Grumbach and Anna Quindlen.—**Glenda Martin**, Green Valley, Ariz.

From **The Great Books—Because Women Say So!**, first edition

WHERE'S THE GRACE?

Reading to a theme has brought this group to deeper understanding of their topic, and themselves.

The new pastor at our church proposed some interest groups as a means of keeping in touch with each other. She had been an English professor before she decided to go into the ministry at midlife, so it seemed natural for her to propose a book group. But the theme she proposed—"Grace in Contemporary Women's Novels"—was a bit unusual.

The group of feminist women in the church who accepted her proposal were already reading mostly women authors, so for them the idea was a godsend. Now we could share our thoughts in a social setting and gain some spiritual insight as well.

**Grace in Contemporary
Women's Novels
Book Group**
Minneapolis, Minn.

Started: 1992

The foundation:
"Before we could find
grace we had to define
it. We decided it was
a very illusive concept.
Individually we came
up with definitions such
as 'an unexpected
coincidence,' 'good
things happening in
spite of bad circum-
stances,' 'undeserved
opportunity.'"

Of course some authors offered more grace through their characters than others, but after a little practice, we could usually find some grace in even the most morbid plots. We also deliberately built in grace by selecting books that gave us a fictional but real insight into other cultures, classes and races.

We started in 1992. We meet in members' homes once a month, first relaxing informally with refreshments. Then the school librarian in our group usually shares what she looked up on the author's background and her other writings.

Our discussions are open-ended, loosely following some guiding questions we worked out, such as: Do you relate to a certain experience of a character in this book? What caught your imagination or what really touched you? What are the important themes for women in this book? Does this book touch your spirituality? Renew the spirit? Did you find similarities/differences to other books we have read? Somewhere during the two-hour session we read aloud passages that we think demonstrate grace.

We have read many women's novels over the years, and in our search for grace in each one, we have become much more aware of grace in our own lives—which of course was what our pastor knew we would do.
—**Faye Kommedahl**, St. Paul, Minn.

From an article in **BookWomen**, Dec. '97-Jan. '98

BOOK GROUP AT THE LAKE

This once-a-year book group brings together long-time friends for good discussion and enrichment.

**Northwoods Book
Camp**
Northern Wisconsin

Started: 2001, meets
once a year

Plans: "As we talked
about another round
next summer, the
theme of 'Reading for
Peace' was suggested.
Someone in the group
offered to host the
camp next August, so
we left with hopes of
another gathering."

We held our second annual Northwoods Book Camp this summer and we had a wonderful time. We have plans going already for next year.

We are nine long-term, book-reading friends who all went to college together. The idea of getting together to discuss books appealed to us—it would add another dimension to our friendships and would be enriching at many levels.

Everyone seemed well satisfied with our discussions of books on the theme of "Growing older." We took turns leading discussions and filling the group in on author backgrounds/reviews. It worked.

We met at a cabin on a lake in northern Wisconsin. In addition to the mind stretching, we enjoyed walking, taking out the canoe and paddleboat, and swimming.

This haiku, by Mim Warren, one of the campers, illustrates the spirit of the experience:

Water, tranquility
Opening hearts, minds and eyes
Renewed spirits soar.

—**Lavern Schroeder**, Harshaw, Wis.

From an article in **BookWomen**, Oct.-Nov. 2002

ANNIE & BARBIE'S BOOK DUO

This two-women book group adds depth to the reading experience and richness to the friendship.

Barb and I have been reading books together for seven years. It was Barb's idea that the two of us get together. Even though I was a little skeptical, wondering if there would be enough synergy with just two people, our experiences have provided an incredible range of reading, as well as a wide variety of ways to approach our reading discussions.

In addition to more meaningful discussions about the books, we have also gained personally by learning more about ourselves and each other. Concurrently, our friendship has deepened through the trust exhibited in our mutual sharing.—**Anne Gero**, Carlisle, Pa.

I look forward to our dinners (often we surprise each other with a new dish), our glasses of wine, our checking in with each other about what's going on for each of us, and finally settling into our chairs to talk about the book.

Reading books with Annie has been a way for me to think more deeply about the books we choose, to take the time to explore a tangential issue that may come up, and to broaden my own understanding of what reading means to my life and to hers.—**Barbara Kohutiak**, Carlisle, Pa.

From an article in **BookWomen**, June-July 2003

The Two-Women Book Group
Carlisle, Pa.

Different approaches:
• We read aloud.
• We take turns selecting the next book.
• Sometimes we write essays about the books before we get together, then read them to each other.
• For awhile, inspired by Nuala O'Faolain's memoir **Are You Somebody?**, we made lists of experiences that shaped us, then shared them with each other.

QUESTIONS THAT WORK

Good questions help make good discussion. Every group hopes for lively, thoughtful, in-depth discussions when they gather to talk about books. Here are some questions that groups have found work for them. Perhaps they will for you, too.

What struck you most about this book?
In my book group we usually start off by going around the circle answering this question. But people also respond to each answer with comments, so it can take the whole time just to get each person to answer this one question.
—**Marjorie Ferry**, Salem, Ore.

What do you think of the female characters?
The questions that prompt the most avid discussions in our group are ones about the female characters and whether we as women can identify or relate in any way to the female characters. Did she grow and change? Did the author develop her? It's great when we have a book with female characters of different ages....oh, the stories and history that spills from our mouths.
—**Anne M. Jones**, Read and Well Fed group, Effingham, Ill.

Was there a passage in this book that spoke directly to you? Why?
Each book speaks to each reader differently. Not only does this question elicit interesting discussion, but it also is a way for book group members to become better acquainted with each other by sharing what they identified with in a particular book.
—**Vona Van Cleef**, El Paso, Tex.

How does this book apply to your life? What have you learned about the lives of others that you didn't know before?
I don't belong to a book club but when I ask my students these questions, the discussions seem to go deeper and broader.
—**Roxanna Bayer**, Argyle, Tex.

What does this book say about your own life?
In the Mother-Daughter book group, our goal is to use the book to think about our own lives. Here are examples of kinds of questions that do that. (These are from our discussion of **Sarah Plain and Tall** by Patricia MacLachlan.)
What did Anna and Caleb remember about their mother, and what are some of the things we think about our own mothers?
How did Sarah make herself more at home on the prairie, and how do we get more comfortable in new situations?
What did the Whiting family do for excitement, and what are some of your memorable family experiences?
—**Laureen Andrews**, Washington, D. C.

Why do you think the author wrote this book?
I often raise this question in a book group (and in my classes when I use books as a part of the course requirements). I have found that it stimulates very interesting ideas and discussion. It is similar to: "What is the thesis of this work?"—but broader and much more speculative about the author's motivation and hoped-for outcomes for the readers.
—**Anne Gero**, Carlisle, Pa.

What does the cover say to you?
In some of my book groups, we have gotten into interesting discussions when we focus on the cover of a book. Whether the cover design is chosen by the author or the publisher, it's intriguing to look at how the cover is connected to the story. When we discussed "Sula" at a Reading Retreat, I was surprised at the number of different covers. Each focused on a different aspect of the story, and each seemed to be targeted to a different type of reader.
—**Melinda Emery**, Mankato, Minn.

Do you relate to a certain experience of a character in this book?
What caught your imagination or what really touched you?
What are the important themes for women in this book?
Does this book touch your spirituality? Renew the spirit?
Did you find similarities/differences to other books we've read?
These are some of the guiding questions we've developed for our discussions.
—**Faye Kommedahl**, Grace in Contemporary Novels book group, Minneapolis, Minn.

SPRINGBOARDS FOR REFLECTION

When Sara Mohn created **Reading Reflections: A Book Lover's Journal,** *she included a page of questions that she has found work well to stimulate individual writing—and also to jump-start group discussion.*

1. Capture the power and beauty of the language. Record favorite passages and quotes.
2. Characters often mirror people in our own lives. Identify characters who reflect aspects of yourself and the people who live in your world.
3. What are the life lessons to be learned from the book?
4. Explore different perspectives from which to respond to the book.
5. Identify defining moments in the text.
6. If you could take the author to dinner what would you want to discuss about the book?
7. Good authors offer the reader a cast of fascinating characters. Which characters would you choose for your friends?
8. Capture the emotions the novel evokes for you.
9. One of the best parts of finishing a good read is passing it along to others. Are there specific people you would like to read this particular book? Explore your motivations.
10. What about this book are you dying to talk about with someone?
11. Did the book highlight or comment on any social issues? Respond to and react to the perspective offered in the book.
12. Draw connections to other books, music, art, movies, or theater you have experienced.
—**Sara Mohn,** St. Paul, Minn.

For more information about the **Reading Reflections** journal or to purchase copies, look on the web at www.lakeshorereflections.com, send email to sara@lakeshorereflections.com. or write to Lakeshore Reflections, 3385 North Snelling Ave., St. Paul, MN 55112.

part three:
HANDY LISTS

For your reference, here are the Great Books again, listed alphabetically by author and by genre.

The List of Authors contains 233 different writers whose books have been designated "Great." Thirty-five are represented by more than one title, with eight having four or more books on the list: Margaret Atwood, Willa Cather, Louise Erdrich, Barbara Kingsolver, Toni Morrison, Marge Piercy, Sherri Tepper and Alice Walker.

In the Books by Genre list, you'll see that—in the spirit with which we have redefined the term "Great Books"—we've created different genres for classifying the books, ones that better reflect the experiences and reactions of the many readers who chose them. You'll find the titles organized this way:

Adventure—Adding a thrill to life.
Anthology, Essay, Poetry, Novella & Short Story—
Capturing the essence, providing provocative moments.
The Arts—For beauty in our lives.
Biography, Autobiography, Memoir, Diary & Letters
    (BAMLAND)—History takes on a different appearance when
    learned through the reading of women's lives.
Culture Critique—These challenge the status quo.
Mysteries—For a quick escape, try mysteries.
Nature—Honoring this earth on which we live.
Novel—Women read novels more than any other genre. How about you?
Science Fiction/Fantasy—This is not about spaceships but about possibilities.
Spirituality—The journey to one's center follows many paths as one honors being woman.

At the end of Part Three there's a list of many of the major literary awards, which can be useful sources for reading ideas.

the great books

List of Authors

Allende, Isabel. Aphrodite: A Memoir of the Senses
Allende, Isabel. Paula
Allison, Dorothy. Bastard Out of Carolina
Alvarez, Julia. In the Time of the Butterflies
Amatuzio, Janis. Forever Ours
Angelou, Maya. I Know Why the Caged Bird Sings
Arnow, Harriette. The Dollmaker
Arrien, Angeles. The Four-Fold Way: Walking the Paths of Warrior, Teacher, Healer and Visionary
Atwood, Margaret. Alias Grace
Atwood, Margaret. Cat's Eye
Atwood, Margaret. The Handmaid's Tale
Atwood, Margaret. The Robber Bride
Atwood, Margaret. Selected Poems: 1965-1975
Atwood, Margaret. Surfacing
Austin, Mary. Cactus Thorn: A Novella

Babb, Sanora. An Owl on Every Post
Bair, Deirdre. Simone de Beauvoir: A Biography
Baldwin, Christina. Life's Companion: Journal Writing as a Spiritual Quest
Barker, Elspeth. O Caledonia
Barr, Roseanne. Roseanne: My Life as a Woman
Barrington, Judith (ed). An Intimate Wilderness: Lesbian Writers on Sexuality
Benitez, Sandra. A Place Where the Sea Remembers
Bernikow, Louise. Among Women
Blum, Arlene. Annapurna: A Woman's Place
Bradley, Marion Zimmer. The Mists of Avalon
Brand, Christianna. Green for Danger
Broner, E.M. A Weave of Women
Brontë, Charlotte. Jane Eyre
Brooks, Geraldine. Nine Parts of Desire: The Hidden Life of Islamic Women
Bruchac, Carol, Hogan, Linda and McDaniels, Judith (eds). The Stories We Hold Secret: Tales of Women's Spiritual Development
Bryant, Dorothy. Confessions of Madame Psyche

Buchwald, Emilie, Fletcher, Pamela and Roth, Martha (eds). Transforming a Rape Culture
Burnett, Frances Hodgson. The Secret Garden
Burns, Olive Ann. Cold Sassy Tree
Butala, Sharon. Luna
Butler, Katherine Hathaway. The Little Locksmith: A Memoir
Butler, Octavia. Kindred
Butler, Octavia. Parable of the Sower
Byatt, A.S. Possession: A Romance

Calof, Rachel. Rachel Calof's Story: Jewish Homesteader on the Northern Plains
Cameron, Anne. Daughters of Copper Woman
Cameron, Julia. The Artist's Way: A Spiritual Path to Higher Creativity
Campbell, Alla Bozarth. Life is Goodbye, Life is Hello: Grieving Well Through All Kinds of Loss
Canfield, Dorothy. The Home-Maker
Carson, Rachel. The Edge of the Sea
Carson, Rachel. Silent Spring
Cather, Willa. Death Comes for the Archbishop
Cather, Willa. Lucy Gayheart
Cather, Willa. My Antonia
Cather, Willa. O Pioneers!
Cather, Willa. The Song of the Lark
Chang, Jung. Wild Swans: Three Daughters Of China
Cheng, Nien. Life and Death in Shanghai
Chernin, Kim. Re-Inventing Eve: Modern Woman in Search of Herself
Chevalier, Tracy. Girl with a Pearl Earring
Church, Peggy Pond. The House at Otowi Bridge: The Story of Edith Warner and Los Alamos
Christ, Carol. Laughter of Aphrodite: Reflections on a Journey to the Goddess
Christ, Carol. Womanspirit Rising: A Feminist Reader in Religion
Cline, Sally. Women, Passion and Celibacy
Cody, Lisa. Rift
Conway, Jill Ker. The Road From Coorain
Cook, Blanche Wiesen. Eleanor Roosevelt, Volume One: 1884-1933
Cooley, Martha. The Archivist

Craighead, Meinrad. The Mother's Songs: Images of God the Mother

Crombie, Deborah. Dreaming of the Bones

Daly, Mary. Gyn-Ecology: The Metaethics of Radical Feminism

Daly, Mary. Outercourse: The Be-Dazzling Voyage

Daly, Mary. Pure Lust: Elemental Feminist Philosophy

Dangarembga, Tsitsi. Nervous Conditions

Davidson, Cathy. 36 Views of Mount Fuji

Day, Marele. Lambs of God

Delany, Sarah and A. Elizabeth, with Amy Hill Hearth. Having Our Say: The Delany Sisters' First 100 Years

Diamant, Anita. The Red Tent

Dillard, Annie. Teaching a Stone to Talk: Expeditions and Encounters

Dorner, Marjorie. Winter Roads, Summer Fields

Duerk, Judith (ed). Circle of Stones: Woman's Journey to Herself

Dunn, Katherine. Geek Love

Ehrenreich, Barbara and English, Deirdre. For Her Own Good: 150 Years of the Experts' Advice to Women

Ehrenreich, Barbara. Nickel and Dimed: On (Not) Getting By in America

Eisler, Riane. The Chalice and The Blade: Our History, Our Future

Eisler, Riane. Sacred Pleasure

Elgin, Suzette. Native Tongue

Erdrich, Louise. The Last Report on the Miracles at Little No Horse

Erdrich, Louise. Love Medicine

Erdrich, Louise. Tales of Burning Love

Erdrich, Louise. The Blue Jay's Dance

Esquivel, Laura. Like Water For Chocolate

Estés, Clarissa Pinkola. Women Who Run With the Wolves: Myths and Stories of the Wild Woman Archetype

Faderman, Lillian. Odd Girls and Twilight Lovers: A History of Lesbian Life in Twentieth-Century America

Faderman, Lillian. Surpassing the Love of Men: Romantic Friendship and Love Between Women From the Renaissance to the Present

Fadiman, Anne. Ex Libris: Confessions of a Common Reader

Fadiman, Anne. The Spirit Catches You and You Fall Down

Faludi, Susan. Backlash: The Undeclared War Against American Women

Fink, Ida. The Journey

Fitch, Janet. White Oleander

Flagg, Fannie. Fried Green Tomatoes at the Whistle Stop Cafe

Floyd, Patty Lou. The Silver DeSoto

Frame, Janet. Janet Frame: An Autobiography

Forbes, Edith. Alma Rose

Gag, Wanda. Growing Pains

Galford, Ellen. The Fires of Bride

Gawain, Shakti. Living in the Light: A Guide to Personal and Planetary Transformation

Gilman, Charlotte Perkins. The Yellow Wallpaper

Gilligan, Carol. In a Different Voice: Psychological Theory and Women's Development

Godden, Rumer. Kingfishers Catch Fire

Godwin, Gail. The Finishing School

Goldberg, Myla. Bee Season

Gordimer, Nadine. None to Accompany Me

Gordon, Mary. Spending: A Utopian Divertimento

Grace, Patricia. Potiki

Grealy, Lucy. Autobiography of a Face

Griffin, Susan. A Chorus Of Stones: The Private Life of War

Griffin, Susan. Pornography and Silence: Culture's Revolt Against Nature

Griffin, Susan. Woman and Nature: The Roaring Inside Her

Grumbach, Doris. Chamber Music

Grumbach, Doris. Extra Innings: A Memoir

Grumbach, Doris. The Ladies

List of Authors

Hampl, Patricia. A Romantic Education

Hamilton, Jane. A Map of the World

Hamilton, Jane. The Short History of a Prince

Hancock, Emily. The Girl Within: A Groundbreaking New Approach to Female Identity

Haushofer, Marlen. The Wall

Hegi, Ursula. Stones From the River

Hegland, Jean. Into the Forest: A Novel

Heilbrun, Carolyn. The Last Gift of Time: Life Beyond Sixty

Heilbrun, Carolyn. Writing a Woman's Life

Helmericks, Constance. Down the Wild River North

Henley, Patricia. Hummingbird House

Herrera, Hayden. Frida: A Biography of Frida Kahlo

Hoffman, Eva. Lost in Translation: A Life in a New Language

Hogan, Linda. Mean Spirit

Hogan, Linda. Solar Storms

Holman, Sheri. The Dress Lodger

Hudson, Lois Phillips. Bones of Plenty

Hubbard, Ruth and Randall, Margaret. Shape of Red: Insider-Outsider Reflections

Hulme, Keri. The Bone People

Hurston, Zora Neale. Their Eyes Were Watching God

Jiles, Paulette. North Spirit: Sojourns Among the Cree and Ojibway

Johnson, Josephine. Now in November

Johnson, Sonia. Going Out of Our Minds: The Metaphysics of Liberation

Johnson, Sonia. The Ship That Sailed into the Living Room: Sex and Intimacy Reconsidered

Johnson, Sonia. Wildfire: Igniting the She/Volution

Jolley, Elizabeth. The Well

Kingsolver, Barbara. Animal Dreams

Kingsolver, Barbara. The Bean Trees

Kingsolver, Barbara. High Tide in Tucson: Essays from Now or Never

Kingsolver, Barbara. Pigs in Heaven

Kingsolver, Barbara. The Poisonwood Bible

Kingsolver, Barbara. Prodigal Summer

Kingsolver, Barbara. Small Wonder

Kingston, Maxine Hong. Woman Warrior: Memoirs of a Girlhood Among Ghosts

Kohl, Edith Eudora. Land of the Burnt Thigh

Kohzina, Elena. Through the Burning Steppe: A Memoir of Wartime Russia, 1942-1943

Koller, Alice. An Unknown Woman: A Journey to Self Discovery

Konecky, Edith. Allegra Maud Goldman

LaBastille, Anne. Women and Wilderness

Landsman, Anne. The Devil's Chimney

Langton, Jane. Dark Nantucket Noon

Laurence, Margaret. The Stone Angel

Lear, Linda. Rachel Carson: Witness for Nature

Lee, Hermione. Virginia Woolf

Leffland, Ella. Breath and Shadows

LeGuin, Ursula. Always Coming Home

Lerner, Gerda. The Creation of Patriarchy

Levi, Jan Heller (ed.) A Muriel Rukeyser Reader

Lindbergh, Anne Morrow. Gift From the Sea

Lippard, Lucy. Overlay: Contemporary Art and the Art of Prehistory

Lorde, Audre. Sister Outsider: Essays & Speeches

Lorde, Audre. Uses of the Erotic: The Erotic as Power

Lorde, Audre. Zami: A New Spelling of My Name

Lowry, Lois. The Giver

Luhan, Mabel Dodge. Winter in Taos

Lyden, Jacki. Daughter of the Queen of Sheba

MacDonald, Anne-Marie. Fall on Your Knees

Mairs, Nancy. Waist-High in the World: A Life Among the Nondisabled

Maitland, Sara. Ancestral Truths

Maitland, Sara. Three Times Table

Markham, Beryl. West With the Night

Marriott, Alice. Maria: The Potter of San Ildefonso

Martinac, Paula. Out of Time

McCrumb, Sharyn. She Walks These Hills

Meigs, Mary. In the Company of Strangers

Meyers, Margaret. Swimming in the Congo

Michaels, Anne. Fugitive Pieces

Millet, Kate. The Loony-Bin Trip

Min, Anchee. Red Azalea

Minatoya, Lydia. Talking to High Monks in the Snow: An Asian-American Odyssey

Moffat, Mary Jane and Painter, Charlotte (eds). Revelations: Diaries of Women

Moore, Kathleen Dean. Riverwalking: Reflections on Moving Water

Moore, Ruth. Spoonhandle

Morehouse, Lyda. Archangel Protocol

Morrison, Toni. Beloved

Morrison, Toni. The Bluest Eye

Morrison, Toni. Paradise

Morrison, Toni. Sula

Murdoch, Iris. The Sea, The Sea

Murphy, Dervla. Full Tilt: Ireland to India with a Bicycle

Naslund, Sena Jeter. Ahab's Wife

Naylor, Gloria. Bailey's Cafe

Naylor, Gloria. Mama Day

Neely, Barbara. Blanche on the Lam

Norris, Kathleen. Dakota: A Spiritual Geography

Olsen, Tillie. Silences

Ozeki, Ruth. My Year of Meats

Padgett, Abigail. Child of Silence

Paley, Grace and Williams, Vera. Long Walks, Intimate Talks

Paretsky, Sara. Bitter Medicine

Paretsky, Sara. Blood Shot

Paretsky, Sara. Guardian Angel

Patchett, Ann. Bel Canto

Patchett, Ann. The Magician's Assistant

Piercy, Marge. He, She and It

Piercy, Marge. The Longings of Women

Piercy, Marge. Summer People

Piercy, Marge. Woman on the Edge of Time

Plant, Judith (ed). Healing the Wounds: The Promise of Ecofeminism

Plaskow, Judith and Christ, Carol (eds). Weaving the Visions: Patterns in Feminist Spirituality

Plath, Sylvia. The Bell Jar

Proulx, E. Annie. Accordion Crimes

Proulx, E. Annie. The Shipping News

Quindlen, Anna. One True Thing

Rafkin, Louise (ed). Different Daughters: A Book by Mothers of Lesbians

Rafkin, Louise (ed). Different Mothers: Sons and Daughters of Lesbians Talk About Their Lives

Rafkin, Louise (ed). Unholy Alliances: New Fiction by Women

Ramsland, Katherine. Prism of the Night: A Biography of Anne Rice

Rich, Adrienne. What Is Found There: Notebooks in Poetry and Politics

Robinson, Marilynne. Housekeeping

Rostenberg, Leona & Stern, Madeleine. Old Books, Rare Friends: Two Literary Sleuths and Their Shared Passion

Roy, Arundhati. The God of Small Things

Ruebsamen, Helga. The Song and the Truth

Ruddick, Sara. Maternal Thinking: Toward a Politics of Peace

Russell, Mary Doria. Children of God

Sapphire. Push

Sarton, Eleanor Mabel. Letters to May

Sarton, May. Crucial Conversations

Sarton, May. The Education of Harriet Hatfield

Sarton, May. Journal of a Solitude

Savage, Georgia. The House Tibet

Sayers, Dorothy. Gaudy Night

Schaef, Anne Wilson. Women's Reality: An Emerging Female System in the White Male Society

Shelley, Mary. Frankenstein.

Shields, Carol. The Stone Diaries

Shin, Nan. Diary of a Zen Nun: Everyday Living

Shulman, Alix Kates. Drinking the Rain

Shuttle, Penelope and Redgrove, Peter. The Wise Wound: Myths, Realities and Meanings of Menstruation

List of Authors

Signell, Karen. Wisdom of the Heart: Working With Women's Dreams

Sigurdardottir, Frida. Night Watch

Silko, Leslie Marmon. Ceremony

Sinclair, Jo. The Changelings

Sjoo, Monica and Mor, Barbara. The Great Cosmic Mother: Rediscovering the Religion of the Earth

Slonczewski, Joan. Daughter of Elysium

Smedley, Agnes. Daughter of Earth

Smiley, Jane. A Thousand Acres

Smith, Diane. Letters from Yellowstone

Smith, Zadi. White Teeth

Souhami, Diana. Gertrude and Alice

Spark, Muriel. The Driver's Seat.

Stabenow, Dana. A Cold Day for Murder

Starhawk. Dreaming the Dark: Magic, Sex and Politics

Stein, Diane (ed). The Goddess Celebrates: An Anthology of Women's Rituals

Steinem, Gloria. Revolution From Within: A Book of Self-Esteem

Stern, Madeleine & Rostenberg, Leona. Old Books, Rare Friends: Two Literary Sleuths and Their Shared Passion

Straight, Susan. I Been in Sorrow's Kitchen and Licked Out All the Pots

Sullivan, Faith. The Cape Ann

Sullivan, Faith. The Empress of One

Tan, Amy. The Hundred Secret Senses

Tannen, Deborah. You Just Don't Understand: Women and Men in Conversation

Tepper, Sheri. The Fresco

Tepper, Sheri. Gate to Women's Country

Tepper, Sheri. Gibbon's Decline and Fall

Tepper, Sheri. Raising the Stones

Tepper, Sheri. Singer from the Sea

Tey, Josephine. Daughter of Time

Thomson, Amy. Color of Distance

Trapido, Barbara. The Travelling Hornplayer

Tsukiyama, Gail. The Samurai's Garden

Tsukiyama, Gail. Women of the Silk

Turner, Nancy. These is My Words: The Diary of Sarah Agnes Prine, 1881-1901 Arizona Territories

Ueland, Brenda. Me: A Memoir

Ueland, Brenda. Strength to Your Sword Arm: Selected Writings

Von Herzen, Lane. Copper Crown

Wagner, Jane. The Search for Signs of Intelligent Life in the Universe

Walker, Alice. Anything We Love Can Be Saved: A Writer's Activism

Walker, Alice. The Color Purple

Walker, Alice. In Search of Our Mother's Gardens: Womanist Prose

Walker, Alice. Possessing the Secret of Joy

Walker, Alice. The Temple of My Familiar

Walker, Barbara. The Crone: Woman of Age, Wisdom and Power

Walker, Barbara. The Skeptical Feminist: Discovering the Virgin, Mother, Crone

Walker, Mary Willis. Under the Beetle's Cellar

Walker, Rebecca. To Be Real: Telling the Truth and Changing the Face of Feminism

Wallis, Velma. Bird Girl and the Man Who Followed the Sun: An Athabascan Legend from Alaska

Wallis, Velma. Two Old Women: An Alaska Legend of Betrayal, Courage and Survival

Waters, Sara. Affinity

Weiss, Andrea. Paris Was a Woman: Portraits from the Left Bank

West, Dorothy. The Wedding

Wharton, Edith. Ethan Frome

Williams, Terry Tempest. Refuge: An Unnatural History of Family and Place

Winterson, Jeanette. Written on the Body

Wong, Jan. Red China Blues: My Long March from Mao to Now

Woolf, Virginia. A Room of One's Own

Yolen, Jane. Sister Light, Sister Dark

Books by Genre

ADVENTURE

Adding a thrill to life.

Annapurna: A Woman's Place, Arlene Blum

Down the Wild River North, Constance Helmericks

Full Tilt: Ireland to India with a Bicycle, Murphy, Dervla

Talking to High Monks in the Snow: An Asian-American Odyssey, Lydia Minatoya

Woman and Wilderness, Anne LaBastille

ANTHOLOGY, ESSAY, POETRY, NOVELLA & SHORT STORY

Capturing the essence, providing provocative moments.

Anything We Love Can Be Saved: A Writer's Activism, Alice Walker

Bird Girl and the Man Who Followed the Sun: An Athabascan Legend from Alaska, Velma Wallis

Cactus Thorn: A Novella, Austin, Mary

Dakota: A Spiritual Geography, Kathleen Norris

Different Daughters: A Book by Mothers of Lesbians, Louise Rafkin, ed.

Different Mothers: Sons and Daughters of Lesbians Talk About Their Lives, Louise Rafkin, ed.

The Driver's Seat, Muriel Spark

Ex Libris: Confessions of a Common Reader, Anne Fadiman

Gift from the Sea, Anne Morrow Lindberg

The Goddess Celebrates: An Anthology of Women's Rituals, Diane Stein, ed.

Healing the Wounds: The Promise of Ecofeminism, Judith Plant, ed.

High Tide in Tucson: Essays from Now or Never, Barbara Kingsolver

In Search of Our Mother's Gardens: Womanist Prose, Alice Walker

An Intimate Wilderness: Lesbian Writers on Sexuality, Judith Barrington, ed.

Long Walks, Intimate Talks, Grace Paley and Vera Williams

A Muriel Rukeyser Reader, Jan Heller Levi, ed.

A Room of One's Own, Virginia Woolf

Selected Poems: 1965-1975, Margaret Atwood

Silences, Tillie Olsen

Sister Outsider: Essays & Speeches, Audre Lorde

Small Wonder, Barbara Kingsolver

The Stories We Hold Secret: Tales of Women's Spiritual Development, Carol Bruchac, Linda Hogan, Judith McDaniels, eds.

Teaching a Stone to Talk: Expeditions and Encounters, Annie Dillard

Two Old Women: An Alaska Legend of Betrayal, Courage and Survival, Velma Wallis

Unholy Alliances: New Fiction by Women, Louise Rafkin, ed.

Uses of the Erotic: The Erotic as Power, Audre Lorde

Weaving the Visions: Patterns in Feminist Spirituality, Judith Plaskow and Carol Christ, eds.

What Is Found There: Notebooks in Poetry and Politics, Adrienne Rich

Winter in Taos, Mabel Dodge Luhan

Winter Roads, Summer Fields, Marjorie Dorner

Women Who Run With the Wolves: Myths and Stories of the Wild Woman Archetype, Clarissa Pinkola Estés

The Yellow Wallpaper, Charlotte Perkins Gilman

THE ARTS

For beauty in our lives.

Bel Canto, Patchett, Ann

Frida: A Biography of Frida Kahlo, by Hayden Herrera

Girl with a Pearl Earring, Tracy Chevalier

In the Company of Strangers, Mary Meigs

The Mother's Songs, Images of God the Mother, Meinrad Craighead

Overlay: Contemporary Art and the Art of Prehistory, Lucy Lippard

Paris Was a Woman: Portraits from the Left Bank, Andrea Weiss

The Search for Signs of Intelligent Life in the Universe, Jane Wagner

The Song of the Lark, Willa Cather

BIOGRAPHY, AUTOBIOGRAPHY, MEMOIR, DIARY & LETTERS

History takes on a different appearance when learned through the reading of women's lives.

Among Women, Louise Bernikow

Aphrodite: A Memoir of the Senses, Isabel Allende

Autobiography of a Face, Lucy Grealy

The Blue Jay's Dance, Louise Erdrich

Bones of Plenty, Lois Phillips Hudson

Daughter of the Queen of Sheba, Jacki Lyden

Diary of a Zen Nun: Everyday Living, Nan Shin

Drinking the Rain, Alix Kates Shulman

Eleanor Roosevelt, Volume One: 1884-1933, Blanche Wiesen Cook

Extra Innings: A Memoir, Doris Grumbach

Frida: A Biography of Frida Kahlo, Hayden Herrera

Gertrude and Alice, Diana Souhami

Growing Pains, Wanda Gag

Having Our Say: The Delany Sisters' First 100 Years, Sarah and A. Elizabeth Delany, with Amy Hill Hearth

The House at Otowi Bridge: The Story of Edith Warner and Los Alamos, Peggy Pond Church

I Know Why the Caged Bird Sings, Maya Angelou

Janet Frame: An Autobiography, Janet Frame

Journal of a Solitude, May Sarton

Land of the Burnt Thigh, Edith Eudora Kohl

The Last Gift of Time: Life Beyond Sixty, Carolyn Heilbrun

Letters to May, Eleanor Mabel Sarton

Life and Death in Shanghai, Nien Cheng

The Little Locksmith: A Memoir, Katherine Hathaway Butler

The Loony-Bin Trip, Kate Millet

Lost in Translation: A Life in a New Language, Eva Hoffman

Maria: The Potter of San Ildefonso, Alice Marriott

Me: A Memoir, Brenda Ueland

North Spirit: Sojourns Among the Cree and Ojibway, Paulette Jiles

Old Books, Rare Friends: Two Literary Sleuths and Their Shared Passion, Leona Rostenberg & Madeleine Stern

An Owl on Every Post, Sanora Babb

Paris Was a Woman: Portraits from the Left Bank, Andrea Weiss

Paula, Isabel Allende

Prism of the Night: A Biography of Anne Rice, Katherine Ramsland

Rachel Calof's Story: Jewish Homesteader on the Northern Plains, Rachel Calof

Rachel Carson: Witness for Nature, Linda Lear

Red Azalea, Anchee Min

Red China Blues: My Long March from Mao to Now, Jan Wong

Refuge: An Unnatural History of Family and Place, Terry Tempest Williams

Revelations: Diaries of Women, Mary Jane Moffat and Charlotte Painter, eds.

Revolution From Within: A Book of Self-Esteem, Gloria Steinem

Riverwalking: Reflections on Moving Water, Kathleen Dean Moore

The Road From Coorain, Jill Ker Conway

A Romantic Education, Patricia Hampl

Roseanne: My Life as a Woman, Roseanne Barr

Simone de Beauvoir: A Biography, Deirdre Bair

The Spirit Catches You and You Fall Down, Anne Fadiman

Strength to Your Sword Arm: Selected Writings, Brenda Ueland

Talking to High Monks in the Snow: An Asian-American Odyssey, Lydia Minatoya

36 Views of Mount Fuji, Cathy Davidson

Through the Burning Steppe: A Memoir of Wartime Russia, 1942-1943, Elena Kohzina

To Be Real: Telling the Truth and Changing the Face of Feminism, Rebecca Walker, ed.

An Unknown Woman: A Journey to Self Discovery, Alice Koller

Waist-High in the World: A Life Among the Nondisabled, Nancy Mairs

West with the Night, Beryl Markham

Wild Swans: Three Daughters of China, Jung Chang

Winter in Taos, Mabel Dodge Luhan

Woman Warrior: Memoirs of a Girlhood Among Ghosts, Maxine Hong Kingston

Writing A Woman's Life, Carolyn Heilbrun

Virginia Woolf, Hermione Lee

Zami: A New Spelling of My Name, Audre Lorde

CULTURE CRITIQUE

These books challenge the status quo

Backlash: The Undeclared War Against American Women, Susan Faludi

A Chorus of Stones: The Private Life of War, Susan Griffin

The Creation of Patriarchy, Gerda Lerner

For Her Own Good: 150 Years of the Experts' Advice to Women, Barbara Ehrenreich and Deirdre English

Forever Ours, Janis Amatuzio

The Girl Within: A Groundbreaking New Approach to Female Identity, Emily Hancock

Going Out of Our Minds: The Metaphysics of Liberation, Sonia Johnson

Gyn-Ecology: The Metaethics of Radical Feminism, Mary Daly

In a Different Voice: Psychological Theory and Women's Development, Carol Gilligan

Maternal Thinking: Toward a Politics of Peace, Sara Ruddick

Nickel and Dimed, On (Not) Getting By in America, Barbara Ehrenreich

Nine Parts of Desire, The Hidden World of Islamic Women, Geraldine Brooks

Odd Girls and Twilight Lovers: A History of Lesbian Life in Twentieth-Century America, Lillian Faderman

Outercourse: The Be-Dazzling Voyage, Mary Daly

Pornography and Silence: Culture's Revolt Against Nature, Susan Griffin

Pure Lust: Elemental Feminist Philosophy, Mary Daly

A Room of One's Own, Virginia Woolf

Shape of Red: Insider-Outsider Reflections, Ruth Hubbard and Margaret Randall

The Ship that Sailed into the Living Room: Sex and Intimacy Reconsidered, Sonia Johnson

Silences, Tillie Olsen

Silent Spring, Rachel Carson

Sister Outsider: Essays & Speeches, Audre Lorde

Surpassing the Love of Men: Romantic Friendship and Love Between Women from the Renaissance to the Present, Lillian Faderman

To Be Real: Telling the Truth and Changing the Face of Feminism, Rebecca Walker, ed.

Transforming a Rape Culture, Emile Buchwald, Pamela Fletcher, and Martha Roth, eds.

Uses of the Erotic: The Erotic as Power, Audre Lorde

Wildfire: Igniting the She/Volution, Sonia Johnson

The Wise Wound: Myths, Realities and Meanings of Menstruation, Penelope Shuttle and Peter Redgrove

Woman and Nature: The Roaring Inside Her, Susan Griffin

Women, Passion and Celibacy. Sally Cline

Women's Reality: An Emerging Female System in the White Male Society, Anne Wilson Schaef

You Just Don't Understand: Women and Men in Conversation, Deborah Tannen

MYSTERIES

For a quick escape, try mysteries.

Bitter Medicine, Sara Paretsky

Blanche on the Lam, Barbara Neely

Books by Genre

Blood Shot, Sara Paretsky
Child of Silence, Abigail Padgett
A Cold Day for Murder, Dana Stabenow
Dark Nantucket Noon, Jane Langton
The Daughter of Time, Josephine Tey
Dreaming of the Bones, Deborah Crombie
Gaudy Night, Dorothy Sayers
Green for Danger, Christianna Brand
Guardian Angel, Sara Paretsky
Rift, Lisa Cody
She Walks These Hills, Sharyn McCrumb
Under the Beetle's Cellar, Mary Willis Walker

NATURE

Honoring this earth on which we live.

Annapurna: A Woman's Place, Arlene Blum
Cactus Thorn: A Novella, Austin, Mary
Down the Wild River North, Constance Helmericks
Drinking the Rain, Alix Kates Shulman
The Edge of the Sea, Rachel Carson
Gift from the Sea, Anne Morrow Lindberg
Healing the Wounds: The Promise of Ecofeminism,
Judith Plant, ed.
Letters from Yellowstone, Diane Smith
An Owl on Every Post, Sanora Babb
**Pornography and Silence: Culture's Revolt Against
Nature,** Susan Griffin
Prodigal Summer, Barbara Kingsolver
Rachel Carson: Witness for Nature, Linda Lear
Refuge: An Unnatural History of Family and Place,
Terry Tempest Williams
Riverwalking: Reflections on Moving Water,
Kathleen Dean Moore
Silences, Tillie Olsen
Silent Spring, Rachel Carson
The Song and the Truth, Helga Ruebsamen
Teaching a Stone to Talk, Annie Dillard
Woman and Nature: The Roaring Inside Her,
Susan Griffin
**Women and Wilderness: Expeditions and
Encounters,** Anne LaBastille

NOVELS

*Women read novels more than any other genre.
How about you?*

Accordion Crimes, E. Annie Proulx
Affinity, Waters, Sara
Ahab's Wife, Sena Jeter Naslund
Alias Grace, Margaret Atwood
Allegra Maud Goldman, Edith Konecky
Alma Rose, Edith Forbes
Ancestral Truths, Sara Maitland
Animal Dreams, Barbara Kingsolver
The Archivist, Martha Cooley
Bailey's Cafe, Gloria Naylor
Bastard Out of Carolina, Dorothy Allison
The Bean Trees, Barbara Kingsolver
Bee Season, Goldberg, Myla
Bel Canto, Patchett, Ann
The Bell Jar, Sylvia Plath
Beloved, Toni Morrison
The Bluest Eye, Toni Morrison
The Bone People, Keri Hulme
Breath and Shadows, Ella Leffland
The Cape Ann, Faith Sullivan
Cat's Eye, Margaret Atwood
Ceremony, Leslie Marmon Silko
Chamber Music, Doris Grumbach
The Changelings, Jo Sinclair
Cold Sassy Tree, Olive Ann Burns
The Color Purple, Alice Walker
Confessions of Madame Psyche, Dorothy Bryant
Copper Crown, Lane Von Herzen
Crucial Conversations, May Sarton
Daughter of Earth, Agnes Smedley
Death Comes for the Archbishop, Willa Cather
The Devil's Chimney, Anne Landsman
The Dollmaker, Harriette Arnow
The Dress Lodger, Sheri Holman
The Education of Harriet Hatfield, May Sarton
The Empress of One, Faith Sullivan
Ethan Frome, Edith Wharton
Fall on Your Knees, Anne-Marie MacDonald
The Finishing School, Gail Godwin

The Fires of Bride, Ellen Galford

Frankenstein, Mary Shelley

Fried Green Tomatoes at the Whistle Stop Cafe, Fannie Flagg

Fugitive Pieces, Anne Michaels

Geek Love, Katherine Dunn

Girl with a Pearl Earring, Tracy Chevalier

The God of Small Things, Arundhati Roy

The Home-Maker, Dorothy Canfield

The House Tibet, Georgia Savage

Housekeeping, Marilynne Robinson

Hummingbird House, Patricia Henley

The Hundred Secret Senses, Amy Tan

I Been in Sorrow's Kitchen and Licked Out All the Pots, Susan Straight

In the Time of the Butterflies, Julia Alvarez

Into the Forest: A Novel, Jean Hegland

Jane Eyre, Charlotte Brontë

The Journey, Ida Fink

Kingfishers Catch Fire, Rumer Godden

The Ladies, Doris Grumbach

Lambs of God, Marele Day

The Last Report on the Miracles at Little No Horse, Louise Erdrich

Letters from Yellowstone, Diane Smith

Like Water for Chocolate, Laura Esquivel

The Longings of Women, Marge Piercy

Love Medicine, Louise Erdrich

Lucy Gayheart, Willa Cather

Luna, Sharon Butala

The Magician's Assistant, Ann Patchett

Mama Day, Gloria Naylor

A Map of the World, Jane Hamilton

Mean Spirit, Linda Hogan

The Mists of Avalon, Marion Zimmer Bradley

My Antonia, Willa Cather

My Year of Meats, Ruth Ozeki

Nervous Conditions, Tsitsi Dangarembga

Night Watch, Frida Sigurdardottir

None to Accompany Me, Nadine Gordimer

Now in November, Josephine Johnson

O Caledonia, Elspeth Barker

O Pioneers!, Willa Cather

One True Thing, Anna Quindlen

Out of Time, Paula Martinac

Paradise, Toni Morrison

Pigs in Heaven, Barbara Kingsolver

A Place Where the Sea Remembers, Sandra Benitez

The Poisonwood Bible, Barbara Kingsolver

Possessing the Secret of Joy, Alice Walker

Possession: A Romance, A.S. Byatt

Potiki, Patricia Grace

Prodigal Summer, Barbara Kingsolver

Push, Sapphire

The Red Tent, Anita Diamant

The Robber Bride, Margaret Atwood

The Samurai's Garden, Gail Tsukiyama

The Sea, The Sea, Iris Murdoch

The Secret Garden, Frances Hodgson Burnett

The Shipping News, E. Annie Proulx

The Short History of a Prince, Jane Hamilton

The Silver DeSoto, Patty Lou Floyd

Solar Storms, Linda Hogan

The Song and the Truth, Helga Ruebsamen

The Song of the Lark, Willa Cather

Spending: A Utopian Divertimento, Mary Gordon

Spoonhandle, Ruth Moore

The Stone Angel, Margaret Laurence

The Stone Diaries, Carol Shields

Stones From the River, Ursula Hegi

Sula, Toni Morrison

Summer People, Marge Piercy

Surfacing, Margaret Atwood

Swimming in the Congo, Margaret Meyers

Tales of Burning Love, Louise Erdrich

The Temple of My Familiar, Alice Walker

Their Eyes Were Watching God, Zora Neale Hurston

These is My Words: the Diary of Sarah Agnes Prine 1881-1901, Arizona Territories: A Novel, Nancy Turner

Three Times Table, Sara Maitland

A Thousand Acres, Jane Smiley

The Travelling Hornplayer, Barbara Trapido

The Wall, Marlen Haushofer

Books by Genre

A Weave of Women, E.M. Broner
The Wedding, Dorothy West
The Well, Elizabeth Jolley
White Oleander, Janet Fitch
White Teeth, Zadi Smith
Women of the Silk, Gail Tsukiyama
Written on the Body, Jeanette Winterson

SCIENCE FICTION/FANTASY

This is not about spaceships but about possibilities.

Always Coming Home, Ursula LeGuin
Archangel Protocol, Lyda Morehouse
Children of God, Mary Doria Russell
Color of Distance, Amy Thomson
Daughter of Elysium, Joan Slonczewski
The Fresco, Sheri Tepper
Gate to Women's Country, Sheri Tepper
Gibbon's Decline and Fall, Sheri Tepper
The Giver, Lois Lowry
The Handmaid's Tale, Margaret Atwood
Kindred, Octavia Butler
He, She and It, Marge Piercy
Native Tongue, Suzette Elgin
Parable of the Sower, Octavia Butler
Raising the Stones, Sheri Tepper
Sister Light, Sister Dark, Jane Yolen
Woman on the Edge of Time, Marge Piercy

SPIRITUALITY

The journey to one's center follows many paths as one honors being woman.

The Artist's Way: A Spiritual Path to Higher Creativity, Julia Cameron
The Chalice and the Blade: Our History, Our Future, Riane Eisler
Circle of Stones: Woman's Journey to Herself, Judith Duerk, ed.
The Crone: Woman of Age, Wisdom and Power, Barbara Walker

Dakota: A Spiritual Geography, Kathleen Norris
Daughters of Copper Woman, Anne Cameron
Diary of a Zen Nun: Everyday Living, Nan Shin
Dreaming the Dark: Magic, Sex and Politics, Starhawk
The Four-Fold Way: Walking the Paths of Warrior, Teacher, Healer and Visionary, Angeles Arrien
The Goddess Celebrates: an Anthology of Women's Rituals, Diane Stein, ed.
The Great Cosmic Mother: Rediscovering the Religion of the Earth, Monica Sjoo and Barbara Mor
Healing the Wounds: The Promise of Ecofeminism, Judith Plant, ed.
Laughter of Aphrodite: Reflections on a Journey to the Goddess, Carol Christ
Life is Goodbye, Life is Hello: Grieving Well Through all Kinds of Loss, Alla Bozarth Campbell
Life's Companion: Journal Writing as a Spiritual Quest, Christina Baldwin
Living in the Light: A Guide to Personal and Planetary Transformation, Shakti Gawain
The Mists of Avalon, Marion Zimmer Bradley
The Mother's Songs: Images of God the Mother, Meinrad Craighead
Re-Inventing Eve: Modern Woman in Search of Herself, Kim Chernin
Sacred Pleasure, Riane Eisler
The Skeptical Feminist: Discovering the Virgin, Mother, Crone, Barbara Walker
The Stories We Hold Secret: Tales of Women's Spiritual Development, Carol Bruchac, Linda Hogan, Judith McDaniels, eds.
Teaching a Stone to Talk: Expeditions and Encounters, Annie Dillard
Weaving the Visions: Patterns in Feminist Spirituality, Judith Plaskow & Carol Christ, eds.
Wisdom of the Heart: Working With Women's Dreams, Karen Signell
Womanspirit Rising: A Feminist Reader in Religion, Carol Christ
Women Who Run With the Wolves: Myths and Stories of the Wild Woman Archetype, Clarissa Pinkola Estés

BOOK AWARDS

In the Great Books list, we've indicated titles that have received major literay awards. Here's information about those prizes.

Bellwether Prize for Fiction. Bi-annual prize created by Barbara Kingsolver to support literature of social change.

The Man Booker Prize. Awarded annually for the best novel written by a citizen of the British Commonweath or the Republic of Ireland.

Kiriyama Pacific Rim Book Prize. Recognizes books that will contribute to greater understanding among peoples and countries of the Pacific Rim.

Lambda Literary Award. Awarded annually in several categories to the best in lesbian and gay writing.

National Book Award. Annual award given by the National Book Foundation for best fiction.

National Book Critics Circle Award. Given annually in five categories by U.S. book editors and critics.

Newbery Medal. First children's book award in the world, recognizes annually the most distinguished contribution to American literature for children.

Nordic Council Literary Prize. Awarded annually for best literary work from the Nordic countries (Denmark, Finland, Iceland, Norway, Sweden, Faroe Islands and Greenland).

Orange Prize. Established in 1996 to celebrate the very best fiction written in English by women throughout the world. Largest cash prize for women.

Pacific Northwest Booksellers Association Book Awards. Annual prizes recognize excellence in writing from the Pacific Northwest.

Pulitzer Prize for Literature. Awarded annually for fiction in book form by an American author, preferably dealing with American life.

Whitbread Prize. Annual prize for the best novel by an author who has lived in Great Britain or Ireland for more than three years.

ACKNOWLEDGEMENTS

The Great Books list wouldn't exist without the adventurous readers who've participated in book groups conducted by Minnesota Women's Press, Inc. over the past 16 years. Through their insights and enthusiasms, their lively discussions, and their commitment to women's words, these readers have honored the work of all the women writers they've read.

Some of those works they've designated "Great Books," saying to other readers, in effect, that "This book touched us, it stretched our thinking, challenged us, provoked good discussion. It was important that we read it."

We are pleased to share their picks with you. We hope you and your book group will want to read these Great Books, too.

—**Glenda Martin, Denise Scheibe, Mollie Hoben,**
book group facilitators
Norma Smith Olson,
book project coordinator

the great books

MINNESOTA WOMEN'S PRESS, INC.

A Place For Women's Words.
Independent & Women-owned, since 1985.

THE BOOKWOMEN CENTER FOR FEMINIST READING:

THE BOOK GROUPS
inspire lively discussion and creative thought.

BOOKWOMEN MAGAZINE
creates a community of readers who love women's words.
For subscription information, contact us or go to our website (address below).

TRIPS & RETREATS
offer reading adventures away from home.

THE LIBRARY
promotes the work of women writers.

THE CENTER FOR FEMINIST JOURNALISM:

THE NEWSPAPER
provides a forum for women in the news.

THE DIRECTORY
connects readers with women-owned businesses
and women-centered organizations.

MINNESOTA WOMEN'S PRESS, INC.
771 Raymond Avenue • St. Paul, Minnesota 55114
(651) 646-3968
books@womenspress.com
www.womenspress.com